The Body Camp

FOOD BIBLE

The only plant based recipe book you'll ever need.
(Well until we release a new one...)

By Ben Whale

Photography by Sofia Gomez Fonzo

CONTENTS

INTRODUCTION

This is a book about plants and plant-based eating. It will show you how exciting, fun and sexy vegetables can be to cook with. Whether this is your first foray into plant-based cooking or you are a seasoned pro (excuse the pun), with the right equipment and a few tricks of the trade that I'll share with you over the course of this book, you'll be equipped with an arsenal of amazing plant-based creations which will blow you, your friends and family away...

If you don't yet know your Tempeh from your Tahini you can refer to our "essentials" list of plant-based ingredients, cooking methods and fool-proof guides from Fermenting to Sprouting. We've designed our recipes to include many of the same ingredients to show you just how versatile plant-based produce can be, without breaking the bank.

Peppered between delicious and nutritionally dense recipes that require little preparation and boast short cooking times, expect to find a few more complex dishes that will satisfy even the most adventurous chefs. Featuring a few extra steps, they require a little more time and organization but are still designed to be easy to follow. Once you've mastered the basics (chopping, roasting and whizzing), you'll be whipping them up in no time at all.

Rather than delving too deeply into the benefits of including more fruits and vegetables into our diets or explaining why we should be minimizing our consumption of processed foods and animal-based products (you can come to The Body Camp for that!), our Food Bible aims to simply empower you with the tools, techniques you need to make healthier food choices.

We hope you enjoy our recipes as much as we have creating them!

Ben and The Body Camp team x

ABOUT BEN

Born in the South-west of England on a small family farm surrounded with cattle, chickens and pigs, and subsequently raised in a country pub I've always been involved with food and where it comes from. I spent many Sundays with my father peeling, chopping and preparing the vegetables for the Pub's famous Sunday roasts, and you could say that this is where my culinary career began.

Having had an affinity for the natural world from a young age I went on to study Marine Biology at college but continued to work part-time in butchers and kitchens. Eventually I came to realize my calling lay in cooking. I left college to take up an apprenticeship in the kitchen and never looked back. Since then my career has taken me all over the world working in restaurants, as a private chef, on retreats, and at weddings, events and festivals where I've cooked for hundreds of hungry campers from make-shift kitchens in tents or vans, and this year I designed the plant-based menu for Royal Ascot. I feel incredibly grateful to have explored so much of the world and met so many inspiring people along the way, and that I actually get paid to do what I love. This book draws on many of the ingredients, methods and flavours I encountered on my travels and is the culmination of the cultures I've been lucky enough (and sometimes brave enough) to explore with my taste buds.

Drawn to the rainbow of colour, crunch and scents I've always eagerly awaited my vegetable deliveries at work, so it wasn't exactly a surprise when plant-based cooking peaked my interest. Keen to expand my knowledge I sought work in a vegetarian restaurant where to my surprise, we still used a lot of dairy, refined sugars and deep fat-fryers. This no longer connected with my values. I accepted a job at a health and fitness retreat and was thrown from the proverbial pan into the fire.

Working in the kitchen by myself I would have to come up with healthy new dishes every day without the ingredients I'd become so accustomed to using (sugar, cream, butter). Coming up with alternative ways to prepare food that looked and tasted "naughty" but was actually super healthy and nutritious presented me with a new challenge and an opportunity to get more creative with my food. I soon realised that it wasn't even hard to do. My secret? Sourcing great ingredients and allowing them to speak for themselves.

This inspired my decision to study nutrition. I wanted to learn the science behind different foods and their effects on the body and understand how to put them together to promote optimal health and wellbeing. Since then sharing the life-changing power of plant-based eating has become a bit of an obsession.

That's me in a nut shell. If you'd like to learn more, you'll find me cooking up a storm on camp...

Essentials

ESSENTIALS

This may look like a big list but don't worry, you don't have to go out and buy it all at once. While I like to have all these ingredients at hand so that I can cook and experiment freely, if you're new to plant-based eating I would suggest that you pick a few recipes you like from the book and build your own essentials list from there.

NUTS AND SEEDS

Almonds
Great for so many recipes! Use them ground as a flour replacement, for nut milk, nut butter or just eat them as they are. Almonds are seriously packed full of vitamins and minerals essential for optimal health and are good for bone health, skin and have been linked with helping to reduce heart disease.

Cashews
Roasted, toasted or blended into cheese, this nut is super versatile and can be used in so many ways! Full of minerals like magnesium and manganese they're great for muscle recovery.

Chia Seeds
These are packed full of protein and omega 3 fatty acids, perfect for maintaining a strong healthy body. They are great as an egg replacement for pancakes or waffles or in raw jams and mousses!

Hazelnuts
I love these in muesli or made into nut butter, perfect for Notella. Used by ancient Greeks as treatments for coughs and baldness.

Hemp Seeds
A great source of protein. Can be used in salads and shakes or as a super healthy garnish on porridge or cereals.

Pecans
Great in muesli or in sweet treats. A good source of magnesium to help those exercised muscles to recover.

Pumpkin Seeds
Another very versatile seed I use in a lot of dishes. A good source of zinc and magnesium.

Sesame Seeds
I often use these as garnish. They are an awesome source of calcium!

Sunflower Seeds
Yet another good source of magnesium. They don't have too strong a flavour until they are toasted, so are great for carrying other flavours in recipes for crackers or raw bread.

Walnuts
Used for savoury and sweet dishes throughout this book these versatile nuts taste delicious sprinkled on top of anything from salads to caramel slices! They contain several unique antioxidants that are only found in a handful of other foods like quinoa and tahini.

BEANS, LEGUMES AND GRAINS

Adzuki Beans
I use these all the time and they are a great source of protein, carbohydrates, fibre, and an assortment of vitamins and minerals. They have a high protein content which can make you feel fuller for longer.

Chickpeas
Use them in salads, curries, stews or blitz them into hummus. They are super versatile and have a great mix of macro nutrients.

Lentils

A great source of protein, fibre and minerals. They can be used in salads, curries, made into dahl or mixed into rice's and other grains to complete the full amino acid spectrum you need to build strong healthy muscles.

Nut butter

I always have a variety of nut butters in my kitchen and use them in smoothies, shakes, chocolates and salad dressings or on a cheeky oat cake with marmite and avocado!

Oats

Smoothies, granolas, granola bars, muesli, protein balls, porridge, you'll find this kitchen staple in many of The Body Camp recipes. Full of fibre they're great little helpers when it comes to clearing out toxins.

Quinoa

A tiny grain that packs a punch it contains a lot of the amino acids your body needs to build and repair. It's a great flavour carrier. I like to use it in salads or as a rice replacement.

Rice

I love rice. What rice I use depends on the dish. If I'm after an aromatic flavour I'll use white rice but if I'm looking for something substantial that will fill me up I tend to use brown.

Soba Noodles

Made from buckwheat (which doesn't contain gluten, the name is a little misleading!). Super quick and easy to prepare, which is handy as I've developed a bit of an addiction.

Tahini

Another addiction of mine! Add it to dressings, hummus or sweet treats instead of nut butter.

SUPERFOODS

Cacao powder and cacao nibs

A super source of magnesium and a great hormone balancer with the essence of chocolate. It's also an aphrodisiac…

Goji Berries

Packed with vitamin C and amino acids to aid your muscles! Delicious in smoothies, granola and protein balls.

Lucuma powder

I use it to sweeten my smoothies. Lucuma contains lots of vitamins and minerals and it's great for your immune system.

Maca Powder

This is used in Peru to enhance fertility and sex drive but also stamina when training. It has a lovely oaty taste, I use it in smoothies with banana and cacao or in granola.

Maqui

A powerful antioxidant that'll help protect your body from free radicals. Best used fresh or as a powder in smoothies, or anything that would benefit from a little acidity. It'll turn whatever you add it to a lovely purple colour too!

Matcha

Helps lower bad cholesterol and is a great detoxifier. Beware, boiling water will destroy it's many befits and give it a grassy taste. Allow boiling water to stand for five minutes before adding it to your Matcha, buy organic if you can.

Spirulina powder

Packed full of minerals Spirulina is nearly 50% protein. Arguably not the best tasting superfood but taken in capsules or added to a smoothie or protein balls it's perfect! It'll turn anything you mix it with a spectacular shade of green.

HERBS AND SPICES

Agar Agar
Made from seaweed. It helps to set food like gelatin.

Arrow Root
Used to help thicken sauces, it's very similar to corn flour. Arrow Root is also famed for its use in the old-fashioned pub game shove ha'penny, where it helps the coins slide along the slate. I have great memories of playing it with my dad when I was little!

Basil
One of my all-time favourites! An antioxidant it protects the liver, and tastes great too!

Black Pepper
Crammed full of vitamins and minerals like vitamin C and A black pepper helps remove free radicals from the body. When combined with turmeric it improves the body's absorption by up to 70% increasing the healing properties of the spice.

Cinnamon
Cinnamon can be used in savoury and sweet dishes to give them an extra boost in flavour. It has anti-inflammatory properties and is known to help prevent and treat of candida.

Coriander
Truly divisive, people either love it or hate it. I love it in curries and tacos. Coriander promotes healthy bones and can aid bad breath and healing ulcers.

Curry powder 'Madras'
Pairs perfectly with coconut-based and is chock-full of minerals.

Ground Coriander Seeds
Can help protect against cardiovascular disease, lower bad cholesterol and calm digestive upset.

Ground Cumin
Delicious with smoked paprika, perfect with ground coriander. Cumin aids digestion by stimulating the salivary gland and the secretion of bile (acids and enzymes responsible for the complete digestion of food). It's also a carminative which means it is good for gas and bloating.

Ground Turmeric
As well as turning everything it comes into contact with yellow (including you if you're cooking with it, use gloves!) turmeric contains lots of bioactive compounds with powerful medicinal properties and like spirulina you could write a book on its benefits. A great anti-inflammatory, it increases the antioxidant capacity of the body and can help prevent and treat cancer.

Miso
Made from fermented soy beans, you can also find miso made from chickpeas, rice or lentils.

Orange Blossom
Made from the flowers of blossoming orange trees it gives a lovely aromatic flavour to food.

Oregano
Full of antioxidants oregano has powerful antibacterial and anti-fungal properties and is used in in the treatment of candida. Add it to salads, tomato sauces and roasted veggies.

Parsley
Like coriander, immune-boosting parsley helps improve bone health due to its high mineral content. Chop it up and sprinkle on salads for an extra nutritional boost.

Psyllium Husk
A fibre made from plant seeds that is used to give elasticity to wraps, it'll help stop them cracking when you roll them.

Rosemary
One of the earliest documented uses for rosemary is to boost memory, intelligence and focus! I love it with roasted vegetables and stews. It has impressive antibacterial qualities and can be used to combat bacterial infections, gas and bloating.

Smoked Paprika
A good source of iron smoked paprika aids your cellular metabolism. I love its soft smokey taste.

Tamari
I use this a lot to season my dishes. It tastes just like soy sauce with the added bonus of being wheat-free so it's a great alternative if you have celiac disease.

Tapioca Starch
A thickener to help emulsify fats with water so they don't separate.

Thyme
Anti-fungal, aids in heart health and provides stress relief when inhaled. It's also delicious.

FRIDGE STAPLES

Avocados
Rich in fat soluble and water- soluble vitamins like A, E, K and vitamin A and B, high in mineral content with potassium, magnesium, iron and a good source of amino acids. Avocados are amazing! I use them on salads and in smoothies, ice cream and bread, you can even bake them or grill them. They freeze really well, make sure to chop them up first.

Broccoli
Broccoli contains vitamin C, K and calcium, as well as a lot of other important vitamins and minerals which boast many benefits including promoting bone health. It's high fibre content helps eliminate toxins in the digestive tract too.

Berries
Full of flavour a handful of berries will add a healthy dose of antioxidants to any sweet dish.

Carrots
Great raw or cooked in stocks, soups, stews, roasted and julienned – and (in the voice of Bugs Bunny) that's not all folks! The list is endless. Carrots contain beta carotene (aka vitamin A) and a whole host of other vitamins essential for optimal health.

Chilies
Chilies release endorphins that will help boost your immune system as well as your mood. Packed with vitamins and minerals a pinch of chopped or dried chili will give you more than just a spicy kick to your food.

Cucumber
Hydrating and alkalizing cucumbers can help reduce inflammation and contain a good amount of potassium that can help lower or maintain a healthy blood pressure. Cut into crudités, add to salads and juices or pair with mint in your water.

Garlic
Garlic has many proven medicinal benefits and is known to help reduce blood pressure and for its anti-bacterial and anti-parasitic properties.

Lemons and limes
It's always handy to have a few of these kicking around to use in juices, dressings, garnishes. They contain a good number of antioxidants in the form of vitamin C, which is needed in the production of collagen for smooth, healthy and happy skin.

Onions
Onions form the foundations for many of the recipes in this from soups, to stews and curries. They contain chromium which aids in stabilizing the blood sugar levels and for centuries have been used to treat inflammation, heal infection, strengthen the immune system and lower blood pressure.

Plant based milks
Best made fresh, but if you prefer to buy yours check the ingredients list before you do. If you see a list of numbers, sugars or any unusual words you're not sure of, don't buy it. A milk made with the nut, water and a pinch of salt (perhaps a touch of Tapioca too) is all you need.

Red Peppers
Cooked, raw or roasted I always have some red peppers around ready to eat raw or toss into salads! Roast and blend with walnuts and tahini to make a delicious dip. They contain vitamin C and recent research suggests they can help increase your metabolism without raising your heart rate or blood pressure! Red bell peppers are a good source of B6 and folate, good for preventing anemia.

Salad of any kind
An easy way to add fibre and of vitamins and minerals into your diet!

Spinach
High in fibre and filled with vitamins, minerals and folic acid which is used to produce and maintain healthy cells. Chuck a handful cooked or raw into smoothies, juices and salads.

Sweet potatoes
Nutritious and delicious you'll find these sweet, sweet potatoes in lots of The Food Bible recipes. Studies suggest eating them with good fats will help with the absorption of vitamin A. They are also a good source of minerals, vitamin C and vitamin B6 which helps reduce the chemical homocysteine.

Tempeh
Crammed with cholesterol combatting niacin as well as vitamin B(s), K, D and lots of minerals Tempeh is made from crushed fermented soy beans so it's also a probiotic. Marinate in Tamari and pan fry for one of my favourite snacks.

Tofu
Shrouded in controversy there are studies both for and against the consumption of Tofu but it's an excellent source of plant-based protein. My advice: make sure you buy organic because the majority of soy-based products are GMO and eating genetically modified food undermines many of the reasons I advocate a plant-based diet.

FREEZER

Garlic and ginger paste
Use a 50/50 ratio and blend and freeze in portions ready to be pop into curries or marinades.

Frozen fruits
Perfect to use these in smoothies, ice creams and sorbets I freeze all my excess fruit before it goes off; banana, berries, melon, avocado…the list is endless! I also use them to naturally sweeten my recipes.

Frozen peas
Up your vitamin and mineral intake adding peas into soups, stews and curries.
Frozen spinach
Great to chuck into smoothies and soups. Whizz in a blender with a bit of coconut milk to make your Thai green curry really green!

Protein balls
I always keep some in the freezer, ready for when I need a quick fix.

Stocks
It's a good idea to cook and freeze your stock in 500ml containers ready to add to soups, curries and stews.

Sauces
If you've made too much sauce or just like to be organised, you can make big batches of sauce and freeze them for a later date.

DEHYDRATING
Not an ingredient or an "essential", a Food Dehydrator is a device that removes moisture from food to aid in its preservation and you'll see it pop up in various recipies throughout this book.

If you don't have or don't want to buy a dehydrator you can use your oven to achieve the same results. Simply follow the recipes instructions and pop whatever you're dehydrating in the oven at the same temperature for the same amount of time, leaving the oven door open to allow the moisture to escape. Make sure it's only a open a fraction, otherwise the heat will escape and your food won't dry!

Note that dehydrators and ovens all have there own personalities so some will dry faster than others and temperature and times may need to be adjusted slightly.

Activating, sprouting & fermenting

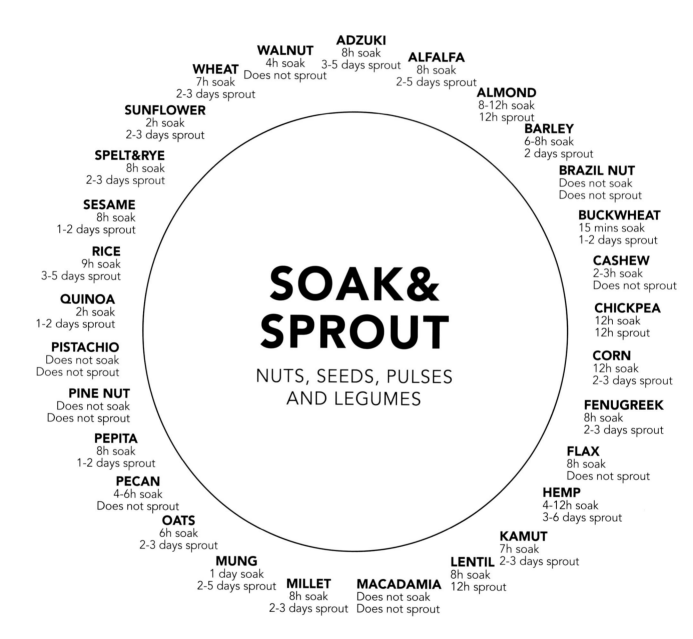

SOAK & SPROUT

NUTS, SEEDS, PULSES AND LEGUMES

ADZUKI
8h soak
3-5 days sprout

WALNUT
4h soak
Does not sprout

WHEAT
7h soak
2-3 days sprout

ALFALFA
8h soak
2-5 days sprout

ALMOND
8-12h soak
12h sprout

SUNFLOWER
2h soak
2-3 days sprout

BARLEY
6-8h soak
2 days sprout

SPELT&RYE
8h soak
2-3 days sprout

BRAZIL NUT
Does not soak
Does not sprout

SESAME
8h soak
1-2 days sprout

BUCKWHEAT
15 mins soak
1-2 days sprout

RICE
9h soak
3-5 days sprout

CASHEW
2-3h soak
Does not sprout

QUINOA
2h soak
1-2 days sprout

CHICKPEA
12h soak
12h sprout

PISTACHIO
Does not soak
Does not sprout

CORN
12h soak
2-3 days sprout

PINE NUT
Does not soak
Does not sprout

FENUGREEK
8h soak
2-3 days sprout

PEPITA
8h soak
1-2 days sprout

FLAX
8h soak
Does not sprout

PECAN
4-6h soak
Does not sprout

HEMP
4-12h soak
3-6 days sprout

OATS
6h soak
2-3 days sprout

KAMUT
7h soak
2-3 days sprout

MUNG
1 day soak
2-5 days sprout

LENTIL
8h soak
12h sprout

MILLET
8h soak
2-3 days sprout

MACADAMIA
Does not soak
Does not sprout

ACTIVATING AND SPROUTING

SOAKING & ACTIVATING

Phytic acid is essentially natures preservative, keeping vitamins, minerals and enzymes in a dormant state until it's washed away by rainfall. Soaking nuts, seeds, pulses and legumes replicates this natural process and removes phytic acid and any anti-nutrients trapped inside them, activating the goodies we want to access and making them easier for us to digest and absorb. New evidence suggests that phytic acid can help withdraw toxins trapped in the body but for me the benefits of removing it outweigh this. Take note of how your body feels after eating your activated nuts, seeds, pulses and legumes and decide for yourself.

SPROUTING

Similar to seeds germinating in soil after rainfall, sprouting is what happens after soaking. The difference being that we sprout our seeds in special sprouting jars, towers or in a bowl. Sprouted foods are great because, as before, the phytic acid has been removed and the "life force energy" released. This multiplies the number of enzymes and increases the nutritional value of the sprout. It's also a really fun and easy activity to do with the kids, they'll love it!

INSTRUCTIONS

Step 1: Follow the soaking times listed in the chart.

Step 2: Rinse and drain well and leave on your rack, tower or in a bowl. Cover with a breathable cloth if using a bowl to keep any little visitors out and leave near a sink (if possible) so that it's easy to rinse and drain again later.

Step 3: Rinse the seeds under cold water at least 3 - 4 times during the sprouting process to refresh them and wash away any bacteria that could cause them to spoil. Every 4 - 6 hours should do the trick. Leave to drain and grow.

Step 4: After a day or two, depending on conditions, you will notice little shoots appearing. Give them a final rinse under cold water and pop them in the fridge. This will stop further growing. Sprinkle or mix them into salads, soups, curries or eat them by themselves, however you prefer.

NOTES

It is important to rinse your sprouts well because the atmosphere they need to grow is also the perfect atmosphere for bacteria to thrive. Rinsing will wash away any naughty bacteria trying to turn your sprouts mouldy. (Remember, if in doubt chuck it out!)

Not all seeds are created equal, some don't sprout - use the chart to check.

Only fill your jars half-full with sprouting seeds, they need the room expand and grow!

FERMENTED FOODS – THE TASTIEST PROBIOTICS!

Fermented foods are delicious, super easy to make and boast an impressive host of health benefits including the ability help strengthen your immune system by the release of cell stimulating and inflammatory molecules. In my mind, fermented foods are absolutely essential for a healthy body and mind.

Generally speaking fermented foods have a higher nutritional value compared with raw vegetables and our bodies find them easier to digest and breakdown, which means we can absorb more of the vitamin and mineral content. They are also packed full of good bacteria which are important in keeping your guts happy and healthy. Did you know there are more bacteria living in your guts than there are cells in your body?

Without a healthy gastrointestinal tract (aka your digestive system) you're less able to absorb the vital nutrients from the food you eat efficiently. An unhealthy gut can cause all sorts of problems. Recent studies have even shown that gut health to correlate directly with your mental health, how amazing is that!

Alcohol, antibiotics, smoking, constant stress, eating the same foods over and over again and not eating enough prebiotics foods like bananas, asparagus, Jerusalem artichoke, oats, lentils, chickpeas, onions, garlic and nuts can all effect the balance of the microbiome found in your gut. Repetitive eating habits limit the variety of bacteria that lives inside it, changing the way in which food is broken down and absorbed through your GI tract.

Eating a varied diet of fresh and fermented food helps the good bacteria you need in your bowel and GI tract to thrive, meaning you'll have more workers in there making sure things keep ticking along smoothly!

NOTES

If you were wondering, the difference between probiotics and prebiotics is that probiotics are the bacteria which populate our guts and prebiotics are foods which help feed the bacteria present in our guts.

Breakfasts

BLUEBERRY & BANANA PANCAKES

Serves 4

PANCAKES

4 Ripe peeled organic bananas
1 Tablespoon maple syrup
½ Teaspoon cinnamon
¼ Cup chopped pecans
1 Cup of organic blueberries

Step 1: Mash the banana in a high -peed blender until you have a 'batter' like consistency.

Step 2: Remove from the blender and pour into a bowl.

Step 3: Mix in the chopped pecans, cinnamon, maple syrup and blueberries.

Step 4: Divide the mixture into four circles on a dehydrator sheet lined with a non-stick paraflex sheet.

Step 5: Dehydrate for 4 hours at 45°C and then flip over and dry for another 3-4 hours. (See page 26 for an alternative cooking method.)

Step 6: The pancakes should now be a soft and chewy texture. These can now be stored in an airtight glass jar until ready to use for up to one week.

CASHEW & VANILLA YOGHURT

2 Cups of organic cashews soaked overnight in filtered water
¼ Teaspoon of vanilla powder
1 Probiotic capsule
2 Cups of filtered water

TIP

To make the pancake stack add some of the cashew yoghurt onto a plate and then add one of the pancakes on top. Do this until you have a few layers. Decorate with blueberries and bee pollen garnished with baby mint leaves.

Step 1: Place the cashews in a high-powered blender with two cups of filtered water.

Step 2: When the mixture is silky smooth empty the contents of the probiotic capsule into the blender.

Step 3: Add the vanilla powder and blend again.

Step 4: Pour the contents into a glass bowl.

Step 5: Leave in a warm place overnight covered with cling film.

Step 6: The cashew mixture should now look fluffy and aerated.

Step 7: Refrigerate until ready to use.

You can also use the Coconut Yoghurt recipe instead, page 233 in the Fermented section.

GREEN MATCHA CHIA PUDDING

Serves 4

---

2 Cups of organic coconut milk

½ Cup of organic chia seeds

½ Teaspoon vanilla powder

3 Teaspoons matcha green tea powder

¼ Cup of maple syrup

¼ Teaspoon cinnamon powder

Step 1: Pour the coconut milk into a glass bowl and whisk in the vanilla powder, matcha powder, maple syrup and cinnamon.

Step 2: Add the chia seeds and stir well until the seeds are submerged in the milk.

Step 3: Cover and refrigerate overnight.

Step 4: In the morning divide the mixture between four glasses and garnish with coconut yoghurt, mixed berries and bee pollen.

TIP

This recipe will keep for three days in the fridge. It's also delicious with seasonal berries and sliced banana drizzled with some more of the maple syrup.

GRILLED ASPARAGUS WITH MUSHROOMS, WILTED SPINACH AND CASHEW SAUCE

Serves 4

16 Asparagus spears

2 Good handfuls of mushrooms of your choice, all cut in half (I use chestnut mushrooms)

300g Washed spinach

Salt and pepper

1 teaspoon of coconut oil for frying

Step 1: Lightly season your asparagus with salt and pepper and a drizzle of olive oil. Heat up your griddle pan and grill them on a high heat until they start to colour and soften. If you don't have a griddle, you can roast them at 180°C for 10 to 15 minutes instead.

Step 2: Pan fry your mushrooms until golden with a pinch of salt in coconut oil over a medium heat. Set aside for later.

Step 3: In the same pan you used for the mushrooms, wilt the spinach over a medium heat. I pop mine in a sieve after cooking to get rid of the excess water.

Step 4: Assemble the veggies on a plate and drizzle with cashew sauce.

FOR THE CASHEW SAUCE

1 Cup of cashews soaked overnight with a few drops of grapefruit seed extract

4 Tablespoons nutritional yeast

½ Cup of water – or veggie stock also works nicely

Salt and pepper to taste

Step 1: Drain and rinse the cashews

Step 2: Blend in a food processor with the rest of the ingredients until smooth. Season to taste.

MAPLE GOJI GRANOLA

Serves 8-10

---

2 Pears peeled, chopped and cored

1 ½ Cups date paste

½ Cup maple syrup

2 Tablespoons lime juice

2 Tablespoons grated lime zest

1 Tablespoon vanilla powder

1 Teaspoon ground cinnamon

2 Teaspoons fine sea salt or pink Himalayan salt

½ Cup of sunflower seeds soaked in water overnight*

2 Cups of almonds soaked in water overnight *

3 Cups of walnuts soaked in water overnight *

1 Cup of pumpkin seeds soaked in water overnight*

1 Cup dried goji berries

* See page 32 for soaking times and instructions

TIP

Adding raw cacao nibs or other superfoods to your granola will give you a little extra bounce in the mornings!

Step 1: In a food processor mix together the pears, date paste, maple syrup, lime juice, lime zest, vanilla, cinnamon, salt and the sunflower seeds.

Step 2: Process together until you have a rough crumb like consistency.

Step 3: Add the almonds, pecans and pumpkin seeds to the food processor and blend into the same crumb like texture as before.

Step 4: Remove the mixture from the food processor and pour into a glass bowl.

Step 5: Mix in the dried goji berries.

Step 6: Spread the mixture out over two dehydrator trays lined with the non stick paraflex sheets. (See page 26 for an alternative cooking method.)

Step 7: Dehydrate the granola at 50˚C for eight hours.

Step 8: Turn the mixture over and dry again for another four hours.

Step 9: When your granola has properly cooled and dried completely, store in an airtight glass jar. This is important, any heat or moisture could cause the granola to deteriorate. Your granola will keep for around 3 weeks.

MUESLI

Makes lots

1kg Gluten free oats

200g Brazil nuts chopped

1 Cup of pumpkin seeds

250g Puffed quinoa

125g Unsweetened dried banana chips

1 Cup of crushed pecans

1 Cup of walnuts

1 Cup of raisins

1 Cup of freeze-dried raspberries

1 Cup of coconut shavings

1 Cup of goji berries

1 Cup of flaked toasted almonds

Step 1: Place all the ingredients into a bowl and mix them all together.

Step 2: Seal in an airtight container to store. Serve with a plant-based milk of your choice.

TIP

You'll find the ingredients in this recipe are used in many others throughout this book, but you don't have to use them all if you don't have them!

PANCAKES WITH COCONUT YOGHURT AND BANANA

Makes 10

¼ Cup of flax seeds milled

2 Cups of gluten free oats

1 Cup of sprouted and dehydrated buckwheat

1 Ripe banana

1 Cup of plant based milk

1 Teaspoon of vanilla extract/essence/powder

Drizzle of maple syrup

Coconut oil for greasing

Blueberries for garnishing

1 Teaspoon of baking powder

TIP

You don't have to use buckwheat in this recipe. Just add a half cup of oats instead.

Step 1: Blend the flax, buckwheat and oats together until it looks like flour. Add the rest of the ingredients and blend again until smooth.

Step 2: Heat a frying pan over a medium heat with a touch of coconut oil. Spoon your pancake mix into the pan and cook for 2 to 3 minutes on each side or until golden brown.

Step 3: Layer with coconut yoghurt, banana and blueberries and drizzle with a touch of maple syrup.

RAW SUPERFOOD BIRCHER

Makes four bowls

---

2 Cups gluten free organic oats

2 Cups plant based milk

2 Tablespoons of organic maple syrup (add more or less to taste)

½ Teaspoon vanilla powder

½ Dessert spoon maca powder

2 Dessert spoons raw cacao powder

½ Cup of organic cacao nibs

½ Cup of shaved cacao butter

Step 1: Pour the plant based milk into a blender with the maple syrup, maca, cacao powder and vanilla.

Step 2: Blend together until smooth and then pour contents into a large glass bowl.

Step 3: Pour the oats into the mixture and mix well.

Step 4: Cover and leave to soak in the refrigerator overnight.

Step 5: In the morning divide the mixture between four deep glasses or a bowl.

TIP

The mixture will keep for up to three days in the fridge. Add some shredded coconut & raspberries if you want to mix up the flavour.

A great source of energy oats are a great way to start the day and make a perfect pre-workout snack.

ROASTED PEAR AND ALMOND PORRIDGE WITH ALMOND CRUMBLE

Serves 4

PORRIDGE

300g Gluten free jumbo oats

800ml Unsweetened almond milk (or any other plant based milk) plus a splash for later

2 Pears cut in half lengthways with the seeds removed

½ Teaspoon of ground cinnamon

1 Teaspoon vanilla powder or essence

1 Tablespoon of almond butter per portion

Step 1: Add your milk to the oats and soak overnight.

Step 2: Place the oat mix into a saucepan with the vanilla powder and cook over a low heat for at 5 minutes. If it looks or feels dry splash in a little milk until you get the consistency you want.

Step 3: Whilst the oats are cooking dust your pears with cinnamon and bake them at 180°C for 15 minutes or until soft.

Step 4: Pour your porridge into bowls and garnish with the baked pear, almond butter and crumble.

ALMOND CRUMBLE

1 Cup ground almonds

½ Cup flaked almonds

¼ Cup maple syrup

½ Teaspoon vanilla powder or essence

¼ Cup melted coconut oil

Step 1: Place the ingredients onto a baking tray and mix them together with your hands.

Step 2: Bake at 180°C for 10 to 15 minutes or until golden brown and sprinkle on top of your porridge.

TIP

You can cook a big batch of oats and keep them in the fridge for the next few days. Add whatever you fancy to keep your breckie interesting!

SMOKED TOFU BACON WITH POLENTA CAKE AND HOLLANDAISE SAUCE

Serves 4

TOFU BACON

200g Smoked tofu thinly sliced
1 Teaspoon of smoked paprika
1 Tablespoon of maple syrup
1 Tablespoon of tamari
Pinch of salt

Step 1: Mix all the ingredients except the tofu together.

Step 2: Pour the mixture over the tofu and leave to marinade overnight.

Step 2: Warm some coconut oil over a medium heat and pan fry your "bacon" until it dark and golden, flip it over and repeat on the other side.

SWEET POTATO HOLLANDAISE

1 Cup of cooked sweet potato
½ Cup of cashews soaked in water with a couple drops of grapefruit seed extract
4 Tablespoons of nutritional yeast
Little squeeze of lemon juice
Pinch of salt and pepper

Step 1: Bake your whole sweet potato with skin on in the oven at 180°C for 30 minutes until soft and allow to cool down.

Step 2: Peel the baked sweet potato and discard the skin.

Step 3: Blend all the ingredients together until nice and smooth.

POLENTA

4 Cups of water
1 Cup of polenta
1 Teaspoon of salt
½ Cup of nutritional yeast

Step 1: Boil the water over a high heat, turn it down and to a simmer and stir in the rest of your ingredients until thick.

Step 2: Sir for a further 2 minutes and then pour into a mould or or dish to cool.

Step 3: Slice the polenta into your desired shape and pan fry in coconut oil on a medium heat until golden brown.

TIP

Be careful when stirring the polenta, it gets very hot and can sometimes plop out of the pan and stick to your skin! Ouch!

TOFU SCRAMBLE WITH ROASTED TOMATOES AND WILTED SPINACH

Serves 2

200g Tofu mashed up with a fork

½ White onion diced

½ Teaspoon turmeric powder

1 Avocado de-stoned & mashed

2 Tomatoes cut in half length ways

2 Handfuls of spinach

Salt and pepper

Step 1: Season your tomatoes and roast at 180°C for 10 minutes until soft.

Step 2: Warm some olive oil in a pan over a medium heat and fry your onions with a pinch of salt and pepper until they start to colour.

Step 3: Add the tofu and turmeric and cook until everything is hot and well mixed together.

Step 4: Wilt the spinach in a hot pan and season to taste.

TIP

Try using smoked tofu if you like the taste, it adds another dimension to the dish.

WICKED WAFFLES

Makes 8

---

3 Cups of plant based milk

2 Cups of oats

½ Cup of almonds

¼ Cup of chia seeds

1 Ripe banana

1 Teaspoon cinnamon

1 Teaspoon maca

2 Dates

½ Cup of raisins

½ Cup of oats

½ Cup of walnuts

Step 1: Put all the ingredients into a food processor – apart from the half cups of raisins, oats and walnuts – and blend until smooth.

Step 2: Add the remaining ingredients and mix by hand to keep these whole for texture and crunch.

Step 3: Pour the batter into a lightly oiled waffle press and cook for five minutes or until golden brown. Serve straight away with sliced banana and a good spoon full (or two!) of chocolate cashew cream (See "Chocolate Cashew Cream" recipe, page 260 in the Accompaniments section).

Kate went to a martial arts fitness camp in Thailand and got addicted to their waffles. I designed this recipe for her!

TIP

This can also be used as pancake mix. Lightly oil a frying pan and cook the same way as you would a normal thick pancake.

Soups & Stocks

BEN'S POROTOS GRANADOS

Serves 4

---

1 Small butternut squash peeled deseeded and cut roughly into 2cm sized pieces

4 Corn on the cob raw kernels cut off

2 White onions diced finely

200g White beans pre-soaked for 8 hours or 2 tins of cooked beans

3 Celery sticks cut thinly

1 Fresh chilli deseeded and chopped into little pieces

2 litres of vegetable stock

Good handful of roughly chopped basil

Good drizzle of olive oil

Salt and pepper

Chopped coriander to finish

Step 1: Start with a good drizzle of olive oil in a big saucepan and add the butternut squash, corn, onion, celery, basil, and chilli. Sweat over a medium heat.

Step 2: Once the vegetables are soft add the beans and vegetable stock and simmer on a low heat until soft and tender. If using pre-cooked beans just add 1 litre of stock.

Step 3: Season and serve with some freshly chopped coriander.

A traditional Chilean dish I came across on my travels, cooked using fresh, seasonal produce - it's delicious! It's tricky to find the exact ingredients here so I've adapted the recipe.

BUTTERNUT SQUASH AND COCONUT SOUP

Serves 4

---

1 Butternut squash peeled deseeded and roughly chopped

1 White onion roughly chopped

1 Thumb sized piece of ginger peeled and chopped roughly

3 Cloves of garlic peeled and chopped roughly

4 Heaped tablespoons of nutritional yeast

1 Tablespoon of tamari

400ml of coconut milk

1 Teaspoon of ground turmeric

1 Litre of vegetable stock

Pinch of salt

Chilli to taste

Step 1: Start by sweating off your onion, garlic and ginger over a medium heat with a pinch of salt until they start to soften, add the turmeric and cook for a further 30 seconds.

Step 2: Keep the nutritional yeast to one side and stir in the remaining ingredients, simmer over a medium to low heat until the squash is tender.

Step 3: Now add the nutritional yeast and blend until smooth. Have a taste and adjust the seasoning if necessary.

TIP

If you find your soup is too thick add add a splash of water or vegetable stock until you reach your desired consistency.

CHILLED AVOCADO AND SPINACH SOUP

Makes 4 big servings

---

1 Avocado de-stoned and flesh scooped out

200g Baby spinach

½ White onion peeled and roughly chopped

2 Cloves of garlic peeled

1 Litre of vegetables stock chilled

1 Lemon juiced

2 Tablespoons of nutritional yeast

Salt and pepper to taste

This one is tricky! Put it all into a blender and whizz until smooth.

TIP

If you don't have chilled vegetable stock or forget to make it, dissolve a vegetable stock cube in water to use instead.

CHILLED RAW THAI SOUP

Makes 4 big servings

---

2 Young Thai coconuts split open, keep the water scoop out the flesh

2 Limes zested and juiced

3 Cloves of garlic

½ White onion

2 Small tomatoes

1 Inch of ginger peeled

2 Tablespoons of tamari

4 Lime leaves

2 Sticks of lemongrass

1 Tablespoon of curry powder

1 Tablespoon of tamarind paste 'optional'

Pinch of turmeric

Put all the ingredients into a high speed blender and whizz until smooth. Easy!

TIP

If you haven't opened a coconut before you can watch a "how-to" video online, or buy some pre-prepared.

CHILLED ROASTED TOMATO AND RED PEPPER SOUP

Serves 4

SOUP

8 Ripe tomatoes cut in half

1 White onion peeled and roughly chopped

2 Red peppers

Drizzle of olive oil

Salt and pepper

Step 1: Put the tomatoes, red peppers and onion into a roasting tray, drizzle with olive oil and season with salt and pepper. Roast at 160˚C for half an hour or until the tomatoes and onion start to soften and colour. Allow to cool.

Step 2: Blend in a food processor until smooth and refrigerate.

HERBY DRIZZLE

MAKES 1 CUP

Small bunch of basil

1 Clove of garlic

1 Lemon zested and juiced

½ Cup olive oil

¼ Cup of water

1 Teaspoon white miso

Pinch of salt

Blend all the ingredients together! This makes more than you need but is good to drizzle on all sorts of things like grilled vegetables, salads and whatever you fancy.

This recipe makes more herby drizzle than you'll need, but it's great to keep in the fridge and drizzle on grilled vegetables or use as a salad dressing.

TIP

I'm a real fan of gazpacho, it's packed with vitamins and minerals and is super refreshing on a Summer's day. You can also serve it up hot, add an extra splash of water if you do.

CURRIED CAULIFLOWER SOUP

Makes 4 big servings

---

1 Cauliflower roughly chopped, include the stalk

2 White onions sliced into thin half moons

4 Cloves of garlic roughly chopped

1 Litre of vegetable stock

1 Tablespoon of madras curry powder

1 Tablespoon of nutritional yeast

Salt and pepper to taste

Splash of olive oil

Step 1: Add a splash of olive oil to a pan and sweat the onions and garlic over a medium heat until soft and transparent.

Step 2: Add the remaining ingredients and simmer for 15 to 20 minutes until the cauliflower is soft and tender, then blend in a food processor or with a stick blender until smooth.

Step 3: Season to taste.

PEA, MINT AND SPINACH SOUP

Serves 4

250g Frozen peas

1 White onion peeled and roughly chopped

Small bunch of mint with the woody stalks removed

100g Washed spinach

1 Litre of water or vegetable stock

Salt and pepper to taste

Splash of olive oil

Step 1: Colour your onion in olive oil over a medium heat with a pinch of salt.

Step 2: Add the peas and water or vegetable stock and simmer for ten minutes.

Step 3: Remove from the heat and add the mint and spinach, blend until smooth.

Step 4: Season to taste.

I love pea and mint soup as it's so quick and easy to make, with hardly any prep time at all!

SHIITAKE STOCK

Makes 4 litres

5 Litres of water

2 Handfuls of dried shiitake or wild mushrooms

2 White onions cut in half

3 Tablespoons of tamari

½ Tablespoon of sea salt

Step 1: Place all the ingredients into a large saucepan over a high heat and bring to the boil. Turn down to a medium heat and simmer for half an hour.

Step 2: Turn off the heat and allow to cool.

Step 3: Strain through a sieve.

TIP

I always make a large pot and freeze it in containers ready to use on a later date. It's great as a base for ramens and pho.

SPICY BEET SOUP, PISTACHIOS AND ORANGE BLOSSOM WILD RICE

Serves 4 - 6

SOUP

2 Tablespoons extra virgin coconut oil

1 Red onion diced

½ Large leek – make sure you remove the end, cut lengthways and wash thoroughly to remove any soil, then thinly slice

4 Cloves of garlic crushed and finely chopped

2 Inch piece of fresh ginger grated

1 Teaspoon dried cumin

½ Teaspoon dried coriander

½ Red chilli roughly chopped – or a whole one if you like it hot!

4 Large red beets peeled and cut into 2cm dice – set a few of the leaves aside to use as garnish

4 Large carrots scrubbed and sliced into about 8 rounds

1 Can of coconut milk

½ Lime juiced

Salt and pepper

Step 1: In a heavy-based pan sauté the onion, leek, garlic, ginger, chilli, cumin and coriander and salt in coconut oil over a medium heat.

Step 2: When the vegetables have started to soften add the carrots, beets and enough water to cover the vegetables with an extra inch on top.

Step 3: Simmer the vegetables on a low heat for about 20 minutes until the beets feel tender.

Step 4: Blend with a stick-blender or food processor, slowly adding the coconut milk until you achieve a creamy soup-like consistency.

Step 5: Season with salt, pepper and a squeeze of lime juice.

WILD RICE

½ Cup of wild rice

2 Cups of vegetable stock

Pinch of salt

¼ Cup of shelled pistachios

½ Orange juiced

½ Lime juiced

1 Teaspoon orange blossom

1 Teaspoon maple syrup

1 Teaspoon sesame oil

Salt and pepper

Micro amaranth or beet leaves for garnish

Step 1: Rinse the rice well and place in a saucepan with the stock. Bring to the boil.

Step 2: Reduce the heat to a steady simmer and cover the pan.

Step 3: Cook the rice for about 30 to 40 minutes or until the grains have 'burst'. Check every 15 minutes and add extra stock or water if necessary.

Step 4: When the rice is cooked and chewy, drain with a sieve and pop in a large bowl to cool.

Step 5: Spread the pistachios on a baking sheet and roast at 180°C for about 5 to 8 minutes. When cooled, chop roughly and set aside.

Step 6: In a small bowl, whisk together the orange juice, sesame oil, lime juice, maple syrup, salt and pepper and orange blossom.

Step 7: Add the orange blossom dressing and toasted pistachios to the wild rice and mix well. Taste and season salt and pepper or a splash of maple syrup to balance the flavour.

VEGETABLE STOCK

Makes 4 litres

4 Sticks of celery roughly chopped

6 Carrots washed and roughly chopped

4 White onions peeled and roughly chopped

2 Leeks washed and roughly chopped

1 Garlic bulb cut widthways skin still on

2 Ripe tomatoes cut in half widthways

2 Teaspoons black pepper corns

4 Bay leaves

2 Sprigs of rosemary

2 Sprigs of thyme

1 Small bunch of parsley or small handful of parsley stalks

1 Handful of dried wild mushrooms – optional extra

2 Tablespoons of salt

5 Litres of cold water

Step 1: Put all the ingredients into a big saucepan and cover with the cold water, bring to the boil. Once it's boiling reduce the temperature and simmer until the soup has reduced by ⅓. Allow to cool.

Step 2: Pass your stock through a colander over a big bowl to catch it and either use it straight away, store it in the fridge for a couple of days, or portion in containers and freeze for up to 3 months.

TIP

I always make a large pot and freeze it in containers ready to use on a later date. This is great as a base for ramens and pho.

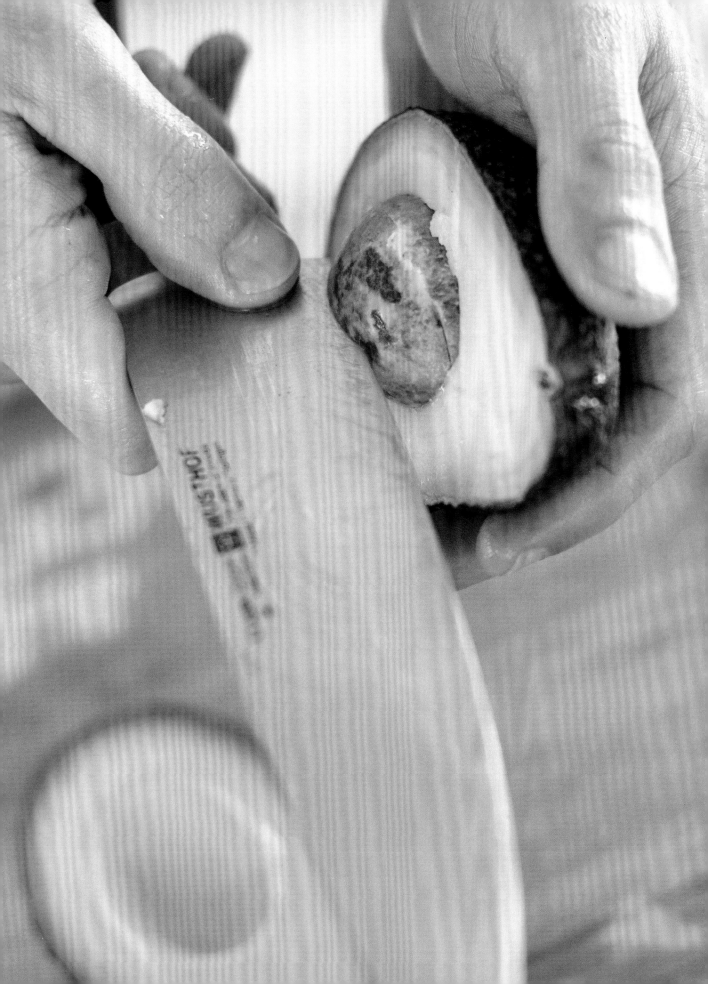

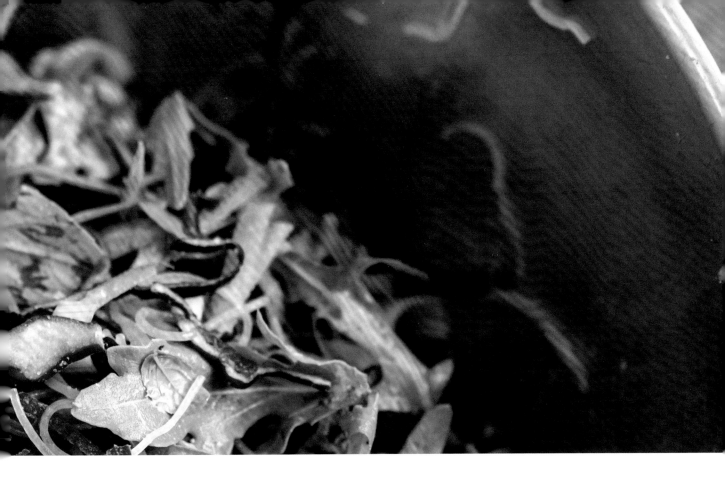

Salads

AVOCADO AND KALE SALAD WITH WASABI DRESSING

Serves 2

SALAD

1 Avocado de-stoned and cut into cubes or slices

10 stems of curly kale washed, stalks removed and ripped into bite-sized pieces

2 Celery stalks

2 Carrots washed and grated

4 Spring onions diced

1 Small bunch of coriander chopped

1 Tablespoon of sesame seeds
Handful of "Crack Nuts" (see page 202 in the Savoury Snacks section for the recipe)

Step 1: Pour the dressing over the kale and massage it in with your hands until it starts to soften. Add the avocado, celery, carrot, spring onion and sesame and toss it together until it is covered in dressing.

Step 2: Sprinkle the crack nuts over the top.

WASABI DRESSING

MAKES ½ CUP

4 Limes juiced

1 Tablespoon of maple syrup

2 Tablespoons of tamari

2 Tablespoons of toasted sesame oil

1½ Teaspoons of wasabi

1 Teaspoon of chilli flakes

Mix it all together and check the sweetness. Easy!

BLOOD ORANGE SALAD

Serves 2

2 Blood oranges or tangerines segmented

Handful pistachio nuts

Drizzle of maple syrup

3 Radishes thinly sliced, use a mandolin if you have one, place in iced water to crispen

4 Handfuls of baby spinach

Step 1: Place the pistachio nuts on a tray and toast in the oven for about 6 minutes. Keep a close eye on them, they should darken in colour and become crunchy but not burn. Allow to cool & roughly chop.

Step 2: To segment the oranges, cut off the top and bottom with a sharp knife. Using downward strokes, slice the skin away from the flesh and discard. Remove any remaining white pith.

Step 3: Place the segments in a bowl along with the spinach and crisp radishes. Drizzle with maple syrup and lemon juice and dress with the chopped pistachio nuts.

TIP

This is a tasty and simple salad that goes really well with the Red Rice and Millet Patties (page 135 in the Mains section.)

LEAN GREEN SALAD WITH LEMON AND MUSTARD DRESSING

Serves 2

SALAD

1 Head of broccoli florets chopped into even sizes

1 Bunch of asparagus hard root removed and cut in half

8 Sun-dried tomatoes chopped into pieces

2 Handfuls of watercress

2 Handfuls of rocket

Small handful of capers squeezed to remove the brine

½ Cup of toasted pumpkin seeds

Step 1: Blanch the broccoli and asparagus for 1 to 2 minutes.

Step 2: Drain the water and put them in cold water to stop them cooking.

Step 3: Toast the pumpkin seeds at 180°C in the oven for 5 to 10 minutes until they start to pop a little.

Step 4: Put all the ingredients into a bowl and add the dressing, give it a good mix and serve!

LEMON HONEY MUSTARD DRESSING

1 Lemon juiced

1 Teaspoon of maple syrup

1 Teaspoon of dijon mustard

2 Teaspoons of olive oil

Salt and pepper

Mix all the ingredients together.

MOROCCAN SPICED QUINOA SALAD

Serves 2

---

2 Cups of quinoa

4 Cups of vegetable stock

½ Cup of dried cranberries or raisins

½ Cup toasted pumpkin seeds

½ Cup of toasted flaked almonds

½ Red pepper chopped into 1cm cubes

Handful of cherry tomatoes cut in half

Small bunch of coriander chopped

Small bunch of parsley chopped

1 Lemon zested and juiced

2 Tablespoons of olive oil

1 Teaspoon of curry powder (more if you like)

Salt and pepper to taste

Step 1: Wash and drain the quinoa.

Step 2: Put the vegetable stock in a saucepan and bring to the boil and add the quinoa. Reduce the temperature to simmer and put on a tight fitting lid. Cook for 15 to 20 minutes until all the liquid is absorbed and allow to cool.

Step 3: Put the rest of the ingredients into a bowl and add the cooked quinoa. Give it a good mix and season.

TIP

Cook more quinoa than you need and store in the fridge, it's a great accompaniment for lots of dishes!

RUBY SALAD WITH GRAPEFRUIT TAHINI

Serves 4

SALAD

2 Raw candy cane beets peeled and sliced into thin feathery pieces using a potato peeler

4 Cups of thinly sliced red cabbage

3 Radishes sliced thinly, use a mandolin if you have one, and put into iced water to crispen

3 Leaves of radicchio roughly torn

3 Heirloom purple carrots (or normal orange ones), thinly slice one into rounds using a mandolin and make the others into thin ribbons using the potato peeler

2 Pink grapefruits segmented with pith removed

2 Tablespoons of pomegranate seeds

1 Cup of mixed dried seaweed soaked for 20 minutes and roughly chopped

½ Teaspoon pink peppercorns

GRAPEFRUIT TAHINI DRESSING

1 Cup of tahini

1 Pink grapefruit juiced

1 Teaspoon maple syrup

Pinch of salt

¼ Cup of water

Step 1: Set aside some of the carrot ribbons, pomegranate seeds, seaweed and half the grapefruit segments for garnish

Step 2: Add the rest of the shredded cabbage, carrot, grapefruit, radicchio, radishes, pomegranate seeds and roughly chopped seaweed into a large bowl.

Step 3: To make the dressing: use a high-speed blender to mix together the tahini, grapefruit juice, maple syrup, and salt. Blend slowly on a low setting until smooth and creamy, adding some filtered water if needed. The sauce should be slightly runny but not watery.

Step 4: To serve spoon a small amount of the dressing onto the salad and toss with your hands to lightly coat the ingredients with tahini. This needs to be a thin coating so as to keep the colour of the ingredients bright, vibrant and sexy.

Step 5: Pool a generous amount of the dressing onto a large-rimmed white plate and pile the salad on top. Garnish with the undressed carrot ribbons, seaweed and grapefruit segments and pomegranate seeds.

TECHNO SLAW WITH TAMARI WALNUTS AND TRUFFLE CREAM

Serves 4

SLAW

5 Medium-sized beets, a mix of candy cane and red

6 Carrots

1½ Cups of red cabbage thinly sliced, use a mandolin if you have one

1 Large spring onion thinly sliced on the diagonal

½ Cup of walnuts

½ Cup of fresh basil leaves

8 Cups of kelp noodles

1 Tablespoon tamari

2 Teaspoons baking powder

2 Tablespoons walnut oil

1 Teaspoon apple cider vinegar

Salt and pepper

Drizzle of maple syrup

Step 1: Soak the kelp noodles in water with the baking powder for 30 minutes to tenderise. Rinse well and chop a couple of times using a pair of scissors.

Step 2: Put the walnuts on a baking tray and cook at 180˚C for about 5 minutes. Remove from the oven and pour over the tamari, mix well and leave to cool. Roughly chop and set aside to use as garnish later.

Step 3: Grate the carrot and the beets and place in a bowl along with the sliced cabbage, kelp noodles and thinly sliced spring onion.

Step 4: In a small bowl, whisk the walnut oil, salt and pepper, apple cider vinegar and maple syrup and pour over the slaw. Gently mix with your hands.

DRESSING

1 Cup of cashew nuts soaked overnight and rinsed well

½ Cup of water

2 Teaspoons white truffle oil

½ Tablespoon fresh lemon juice

½ Teaspoon date syrup

2 Teaspoons tamari

Pinch of salt

Place all ingredients in a high-speed blender and combine until smooth.

TO ASSEMBLE

Spoon a generous amount of truffle sauce onto a wide-rimmed plate. Using your hands, pile the kelp on top of and drizzle more truffle cream on top. Don't be shy with the truffle cream! Garnish with the tamari walnuts and ripped basil.

THAI RAINBOW SALAD
WITH CRISPY TEMPEH

Serves 4

RAINBOW SALAD

2 Courgettes cut lengthways seeds scooped out cut into half moons

1 Red pepper deseeded and cut into thin stripes

½ Red onion sliced thinly

2 Carrots grated (julienne if you have the knife skills!)

300g Green beans

1 Tablespoon of sesame seeds black or white, or you can use both if you like

Step 1: Blanch the beans in salted water for 30 seconds to 1 minute depending on the size of the beans. I like mine crunchy but you can cook them for longer if you like. Drain and put them in cold water to stop them from cooking.

Step 2: Toss all the ingredients into a big bowl ready to add the dressing later.

CASHEW LIME AND COCONUT DRESSING

½ Cup of cashews soaked in lots of water for 8 hours with a couple of drops of grapefruit seed extract

1 Cup of coconut milk

1 Lime zested and juiced

2 Cloves of garlic

1 Tablespoon of tamarind paste

2 Tablespoons of tamari or soy sauce

2 Sticks of lemongrass cut into pieces, just the white parts and stalk removed

1 Thumb of ginger peeled cut into pieces

Drizzle of toasted sesame oil

Step 1: Blend all the ingredients until smooth.

Step 2: Pour over the salad and mix until everything is evenly coated

---

CRISPY TEMPEH

3 to 10 Slices of tempeh

2 Tablespoons of tamari

A small bowl of corn flour to dust the tempeh

1 Tablespoon of coconut oil for frying

TIP

You can get some really delicious marinated tempeh out there which is really good dipped into satay sauce. (See the 'Satay Sauce' recipe, page 270 in the Accompaniments section)

Step 1: If not marinated already, drizzle the tempeh with tamari to season and help the cornflour stick.

Step 2: Put the tempeh into the cornflour and coat it. Pat off the excess flour.

Step 3: Melt the coconut oil in a frying pan over a medium heat, carefully put your tempeh into the pan and cook on both sides for 2 minutes until nice and crispy!

TOFU NICOISE

Serves 2

TOFU MARINADE

200g Tofu cut into cubes

1 Clove of garlic crushed

1 Inch of grated ginger

2 Tablespoons tamari

1 Teaspoon maple syrup

1½ Cups of water

Put the tofu into a bowl, combine the rest of the ingredients and pour over the top. Allow to marinate for at least an hour (overnight is even better).

TOFU COATING

½ Cup of sesame seeds

½ Cup of black sesame seeds

1 Cup of cornflour

1 Teaspoon salt

1 Teaspoon coconut oil for frying

Step 1: Mix all the dry ingredients evenly.

Step 2: Remove the tofu from the marinade and dip into the sesame and cornflour mix so it is coated, pat off any excess mix

Step 3: Heat coconut oil in a frying pan over a medium heat and fry the tofu until golden brown on both sides.

SALAD DRESSING

2 Limes zested and juiced

1 Teaspoon maple syrup

1 Tablespoon sesame oil

1 Teaspoon white miso paste

1 Teaspoon tamari

Mix all the ingredients together and taste. Add more maple syrup or salt as required.

THE SALAD

100g Green beans

6 Spears of asparagus

1 Avocado de-stoned and sliced into strips

10 Cherry tomatoes cut in half

2 Baby gem lettuce leaves separated and washed

100g Rocket or watercress washed

½ Mango sliced into strips

1 Fresh chilli sliced – or half depending on heat and personal preference

Step 1: Blanch the green beans and asparagus then dunk into cold, preferably iced water, to stop them cooking.

Step 2: Once chilled, drain and mix all your salad ingredients together, along with the dressing. Plate and add the tofu. Enjoy!

TIP

You can make a big batch of the dressing and use it for other recipes and salads!

Mains

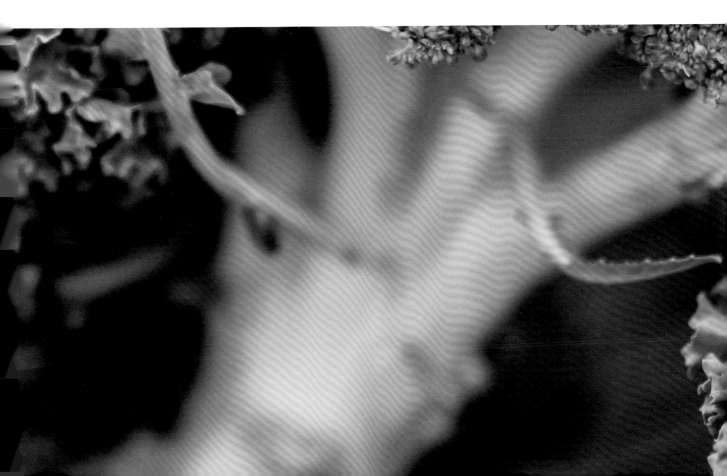

BAKED FALAFELS WITH GREEN CHILLI AND MINT PESTO

Serves 4

FALAFELS

2 Cups of dry chickpeas soaked overnight in filtered water

½ Onion finely chopped

¼ Teaspoon cumin powder

½ Dessert spoon chopped coriander

1 Dessert spoon melted coconut oil

Sea salt to taste

Step 1: Rinse the pre-soaked chickpeas under cold running water and drain well. Dry them in a clean tea towel.

Step 2: Pop them in the food processor and process until roughly blended.

Step 3: Add the cumin powder, coriander and sea salt, and blend again until well mixed and slightly rough in appearance.

Step 4: Check the seasoning.

Step 5: Line a large roasting tray with greaseproof paper and brush with melted coconut oil.

Step 6: Roll the falafel mixture into golf ball-sized pieces and place these on top of the paper.

Step 7: Bake in the oven at 180 °C for around 20 to 25 minutes or until golden brown.

Step 8: Remove from the oven and leave in a warm place until ready to serve.

CORIANDER, GREEN CHILLI AND MINT PESTO

2 Cups of coriander leaves
½ Cup of mint leaves
1 Small green chilli
1 Clove of garlic
1 Dessert spoon nutritional yeast
¾ Cup of olive oil
Sea salt to taste

Step 1: Process the ingredients together in a high-speed blender until smooth.

Step 2: Pour into a glass jar and refrigerate until ready to use.

ASPARAGUS AND BROCCOLI

1 Bunch of green asparagus
1 Head of broccoli
⅛ Cup of olive oil
Sea salt to taste

Step 1: Boil 2 litres of water with a pinch of sea salt.

Step 2: Peel the asparagus and remove the 'woody' ends with a sharp knife, cut into 1-inch long pieces.

Step 3: Remove the broccoli stalk and cut the heads into small florets.

Step 4: Blanch the asparagus and broccoli in the water for about 1 minute, drain with a sieve and run under cold water to refresh and keep the colour green.

Step 5: Dry the asparagus and broccoli on a paper towel. Put into a bowl and drizzle with olive oil and sea salt until ready to use.

When you are ready, use the photo as a guide to assemble your plate. Serve as a starter or as a main course with salad, garnished with sprouts and microgreens.

CHICKPEA AND CAULIFLOWER KORMA

Serves 4

---

4 White onions sliced thinly

8 Cloves of garlic minced

2 Thumbs of ginger peeled and chopped finely

8 Cardamom pods

2 Teaspoons ground cumin

2 Teaspoons of ground coriander

2 Teaspoons of turmeric

1 Teaspoon of chilli powder

4 Bay leaves

4 Cloves

1 Cup of ground almonds

1 Cup of desiccated coconut

600ml Vegetable stock

2 Tins of coconut milk

2 Tablespoons coconut oil

1 Cauliflower florets chopped and cut into even sizes

100g Chickpeas pre-soaked for 8 hours

Handful of spinach

TIP

I serve this with basmati rice and homemade dosa (See the 'Dosa' recipe, page 237 in the Fermented section).

Step 1: Boil your chickpeas for 45 minutes until tender with a small pinch of salt, or use a tin of ready cooked chickpeas.

Step 2: Melt the coconut oil in a saucepan and sweat the onions until soft. Add the garlic and ginger and cook for 1 minute.

Step 3: Add all the spices, bay leaves, cloves, cardamom and vegetable stock and give it a good mix, reduce the liquid by half.

Step 4: Add the coconut milk and reduce again by a third. Remove the cardamom pods, bay leaves and cloves and then blend with a stick blender. Add the ground almonds and desiccated coconut and simmer for 5 to 10 minutes.

Step 5: Over a low heat cook the cauliflower and chickpeas in the sauce for 5 minutes. Stir occasionally. Finish with a handful of spinach and serve.

CHICKPEA FRITTATAS WITH AUBERGINE BACON

Serves 4

CHICKPEA FRITTATA

2 Cups of chickpea flour
1 Teaspoon sea salt
1 Tablespoon nutritional yeast
½ Teaspoon baking powder
⅛ Cup of lemon juice
1½ Cups of water
1 Tablespoon coconut oil

Step 1: Mix the chickpea flour with the sea salt, nutritional yeast and baking powder in a large bowl with a whisk.

Step 2: Stir in the water and lemon juice until you have a smooth batter.

Step 3: Divide the batter into 4 separate bowls.

Step 4: In a large non-stick pan melt the coconut oil over a low to medium heat. Pour in one bowl of batter and cook slowly until the mixture starts to firm and you can turn over the frittata. Cook until golden brown.

Step 6: Pop the frittata on a plate lined with a paper towel and repeat the process with the three remaining portions of batter. Leave to cool until ready to use.

EGGPLANT BACON

4 Large aubergines
2 Teaspoons Himalayan salt

Step 1: Peel and slice the aubergines, cut into long thin slices.

Step 2: Lay the slices of aubergine on a tray and sprinkle with salt, leave to stand for 3 hours.

Step 3: After 3 hours, squeeze the liquid out of the aubergine and wash in water. Dry in paper towels and put into a shallow dish until the marinade is ready.

TIP

All the recipes can be made in advance, which makes it really easy if you're entertaining for friends and family.

MARINADE

1 Dried chipotle chilli soaked in water

Water from chilli

4 Tablespoons maple syrup

4 Tablespoons olive oil

4 Tablespoons tamari

4 Tablespoons apple cider vinegar

2 Teaspoons smoked paprika

2 Teaspoons ground cumin

Ground black pepper

Step 1: Blend all the ingredients together and pour over the aubergine, make sure they are evenly coated.

Step 2: Refrigerate in the marinade overnight.

Step 3: Take the aubergines out of the marinade and lay the strips on the dehydrator sheets lined with the non-stick paraflex sheets so they are flat but not stacked on top of one another.

Step 4: Dehydrate at 40 °C for 6 to 8 hours or until soft and chewy with a 'bacon' appearance. See page 26 for an alternative cooking method.

Step 5: Refrigerate your "bacon" in a sealed container until ready to use.

CASHEW SOURED CREAM

2 Cups of soaked cashews

2 Lemons juiced

Sea salt to taste

Step 1: Combine the cashews and lemon juice in a high-speed blender until smooth.

Step 2: Season to taste and refrigerate until ready to use.

AVOCADO SALSA

2 Ripe avocados peeled and the stone removed

1 Tablespoon chopped coriander

1 Lime juiced

¼ Teaspoon finely chopped green chilli

Sea salt to taste

Step 1: Chop the avocados into small cubes and put in a bowl with the lime juice.

Step 2: Add the coriander, green chilli and sea salt. Mix everything together using a fork so you can mash the ingredients together.

Step 3: Season and refrigerate until ready to use.

Using the photograph as a guide dress the frittata with the soured cream, avocado salsa and aubergine bacon. Decorate with sprouts and serve warm. If you need to, re-heat at 180°C for 5 minutes.

CORN TACOS WITH SPICY TOFU AND CARAMELISED ONIONS

Serves 4

CORN TACOS

3 Cups of organic sweetcorn nibs

1½ Cups of seeded and chopped red pepper

¾ Cup of ground flaxseed

1 Teaspoon chilli flakes

1½ Teaspoons sea salt

1 Teaspoon ground cumin

Step 1: Put the chopped red pepper and sweetcorn into the food processor and blend until smooth.

Step 2: Add the cumin, salt, chilli and ground flaxseed, and process again until the mixture is dough-like in consistency.

Step 3: Spoon the mixture into 4 balls onto a dehydrator sheet lined with a non-stick paraflex sheet.

Step 4: Using the back of a spoon, move the mixture around so that you have 4 circles on the tray around 3 inches wide in diameter.

Step 5: Dehydrate for 4 hours at 45°C. See page 26 for an alternative cooking method.

Step 6: Peel off and turn over, drying for another 4 hours. When ready, store in a cool dry place until ready to serve.

NOTE

Depending on the humidity and temperature of the room, the time it takes for the tacos to dry may vary. I can take up to 6 hours each side whereas in the summer months, they seem to dry much faster.

SPICY TOFU CAKES

200g Soft white tofu

1 Dessert spoon chopped coriander

⅛ Teaspoon smoked paprika

1 Small clove of garlic crushed

½ Dessert spoon melted coconut oil

¼ Teaspoon sea salt

Step 1: Place all the ingredients in a food processor and blend until smooth. Leave in the mixing bowl.

Step 2: Line an oven tray with greaseproof paper and brush with melted coconut oil.

Step 3: Mould the tofu with your hands into small patties about the size of a small golf ball. This mixture should make about 12. Place these on the baking tray.

Step 4: Bake in an oven for 20 minutes on 180°C. When ready, remove and leave to cool until ready to serve.

CARAMELISED ONIONS

2 Medium-sized onions peeled and finely sliced

3 Dates de-stoned

3 Tablespoons tamari

2 Tablespoons water

Step 1: Mix the dates, tamari and water together in a high-speed blender.

Step 2: Once smooth pour the mixture over the onions in a big bowl and stir to coat them evenly.

Step 3: Leave to marinate for 2 hours.

Step 4: Spread the onion mixture over a dehydrator sheet lined with a paraflex sheet.

Step 6: Dehydrate at 50°C for 8 hours or until soft and chewy. See page 26 for an alternative cooking method.

To prepare the tacos, gently fold them in half. Place some fresh organic rocket leaves on the bottom with microleaves and sprouts. Pop the spicy tofu cakes on top and decorate with caramelised onions. Drizzle with cashew soured cream (recipe page 114) and serve.

FULLY LOADED NACHOS

Makes a massive bowl for 2

SERVE WITH SMOKY GRILLED SWEETCORN TORTILLAS
(See the recipe, page 272 in Accompaniments section.)

NACHO CHEESE

MAKES 500ML

2 Cups of cooked sweet potato

1 Cup of water

1 Tablespoon of lemon juice

¼ Cup of nutritional yeast

1 Garlic clove

1½ Tablespoons of arrowroot

Pinch of cayenne pepper

Pinch of smoked paprika

Pinch of salt

Step 1: Roast two sweet potatoes whole at 180°C for half an hour or until soft and a fork can easily pierce the skin. Allow to cool.

Step 2: Peel the skin from the sweet potato with your fingers, it will be too soft to use a peeler. Or chop it in half and scoop out the flesh with a spoon.

Step 3: Blend all the ingredients together and pour into a small saucepan.

Step 4: Cook on a medium low heat stirring continually until it starts to thicken.

TIP

Garnish with fresh chopped chilli, spring onion and coriander - which goes really well with sweet potato.

REFRIED BEANS

MAKES 3 CUPS

200g Dried pinto beans soaked for 8 hours or 2 tins of cooked black beans

4 Bay leaves

2 White onions cut as finely as you can

1 Tablespoon of tomato puree

4 Cloves of garlic chopped roughly

1 Teaspoon of cumin

1 Teaspoon of smoked paprika

Salt to taste

Step 1: Drain and rinse the beans, then put them into a saucepan and cover with cold water leaving at least 2 inches at the top. Simmer until tender, try a few to make sure as sometimes one will be perfect when the rest are still hard. You can skip this step if you use tinned black beans.

Step 2: Whilst the beans are cooking, sweat off your onions and garlic until nice and soft, then add the tomato puree and cook for a further 2 minutes.

Step 3: Put all the ingredients into a food processor and blend until smooth, or pulse if you like it chunky.

GUACAMOLE

MAKES 2 CUPS

4 Avocados de-stoned flesh
scooped out

1 Lemon juiced

Salt and pepper

Chop the avocado roughly and mix with the lemon juice, salt and
pepper.

SALSA

4 Tomatoes diced roughly into
1cm chunks

2 Cloves of garlic crushed and
chopped finely

¼ Red onion diced as small as
possible

1 Lime zested and juiced

8 Sprigs of coriander ripped

½ Teaspoon smoked paprika

½ Teaspoon of cumin

Pinch salt and pepper

Chilli to taste

Mix all the ingredients together in a bowl and season to taste.

PICKLED RED CABBAGE

¼ Red cabbage sliced really
thinly

2 Tablespoons of apple cider
vinegar

Pinch of salt

Put the ingredients into a bowl and mix every 5 minutes or so until
the cabbage softens.

TIP

*To slice the red cabbage I use
a food processor with a slicing
attachment, it keeps it even and
thin.*

MEZZE

SPICED LENTILS

½ Cup sunflower seeds

½ Cup deshelled hemp seeds

1 Cup of dried lentils soaked for 4 hours (depending on which lentils you use)

¼ Cup of raisins or sultanas

½ Teaspoon ground cumin

½ Teaspoon smoked paprika

Drizzle of olive oil

Salt and pepper to taste

Step 1: Heat the oven to 180°C and toast your sunflower seeds for 5 to 10 minutes.

Step 2: Cook the lentils over a medium heat for about 20 to 30 minutes until tender. Drain and rinse with water then stand to allow any remaining water to come out.

Step 3: Once cool and dry, put into a bowl and mix in the rest of the ingredients. Season with salt and pepper. A little chopped coriander is a nice addition too, if you like the taste!

CURRIED CAULIFLOWER

1 Small cauliflower chopped into florets

1 Tablespoon madras curry powder

Good pinch of salt and pepper

Step 1: Preheat the oven at 200°C and then cover the cauliflower florets in the curry powder, salt and pepper until evenly coated.

Step 2: Transfer the florets onto a baking tray lined with greaseproof or lightly oiled paper, and roast for 10 to 15 minutes until they start to go golden.

HEMP AND SUNFLOWER SEED TABOULI

½ Cup of deshelled hemp seeds

½ Cup of sunflower seeds

1 Big handful of parsley

1 Big handful of coriander

1 Big handful of mint

6 Cherry tomatoes cut in halves

1 Clove of garlic crushed and chopped into tiny bits

1 Lemon juiced

Drizzle of olive oil

Salt and pepper to taste

Step 1: Toast the sunflower seeds on a roasting tray for 5 to 10 minutes at 180°C.

Step 2: Chop all the herbs together.

Step 3: Put all the ingredients into a bowl and mix together. Taste and adjust the seasoning if you need to.

TIP

I serve this with baba ghanoush and muhammara. You can find the recipes on page 199 in the Savoury Snacks section.

MUSHROOM BOURGUIGNON

I made this up on a cold, rainy day when we wanted a delicious winter warmer!

Makes 2 big portions

2 Carrots peeled and chopped into chunky discs

1 Onion sliced thinly into half moons

4 Cloves of garlic chopped into thin slices

2 Sticks of celery chopped as thinly as possible

300g Chestnut mushrooms cut into halves or quarters, depending on their size

4 Cups of dried wild mushrooms

2 Cups red wine

5 Cups of boiling water

1 Heaped tablespoon tomato purée

Salt and pepper

Splash of olive oil

2 tablespoons cornflour with a splash of water

TIP

You can double the recipe and make extra to freeze in portions for another day.

Step 1: Make a stock from your dried wild mushrooms by pouring 5 cups of boiling water over them and leaving until cool.

Step 2: Add a splash of olive oil to your saucepan and sweat the onion, carrot, celery and garlic with a pinch of salt and pepper over a low heat until they start to caramelise.

Step 3: Whilst your onions and carrots are cooking, pan fry the chestnut mushrooms in the coconut oil with a pinch of salt small batches. Use a medium to high heat and cook until golden brown then set them aside for later.

Step 4: Add the tomato purée to the carrot, celery and garlic and cook over a medium heat until it starts to stick to the bottom. Then add your pan-fried chestnut mushrooms.

Step 5: Drain the stock you made earlier through a sieve and add it to the pot, you can chop up the leftover mushrooms and add them to the pot or discard them. I don't like the texture and sometimes they have bits of grit in them, so I tend to discard them. Pour in the win and reduce the sauce by half.

Step 6: Check the seasoning and add the cornflour mixed with water to the sauce to make it thicker. It's very important to mix the cornflour with water before you add it to your sauce to stop it becoming lumpy!

CHEESY MASH

400g White potatoes, Maris Piper or similar, peeled and chopped into cubes

4 Tablespoons nutritional yeast

Splash of oat milk or plant based alternative

Splash of olive oil

Salt and pepper to taste

Step 1: Boil the potatoes in water over a medium heat until tender and a knife or fork passes through them easily. Drain in a colander.

Step 2: Place them back into the saucepan with the rest of the ingredients and mash until smooth. Season to taste. I serve this dish with steamed green beans and broccoli.

PHO

Serves 4

4 Litres of vegetable stock (see page 82 for the recipe)

3 White onions cut in half

4 Inches of ginger roughly chopped, skin left on

1 Tablespoon coriander seeds

1 Tablespoon fennel seeds

3 Star anise

2 Sticks of cinnamon

3 Tablespoons tamari or soy sauce

6 Cloves of garlic bashed

1 Cup of dried mushrooms (I use shiitake)

Step 1: Put the onion, garlic and ginger with the skin still on into a roasting tray and lightly cook at 180°C for 20 to 30 minutes until the onion and garlic start to burn slightly

Step 2: Roast the spices in the oven for 4 to 5 minutes until they start to smell aromatic and fragrant.

Step 3: Add all the ingredients to your vegetable stock and boil over a medium to high heat until it's reduce by a third. Taste the stock and season as needed.

I serve this with rice noodles, bean sprouts, tempeh, chilli, bok choy, mushrooms, coriander, lemon and black sesame seeds.

TIP

I think the stock tastes better if you make it the day before you need it. It's also a good idea to double the recipe and freeze it for another day. This will save you time in the future.

QUESADILLA

Makes 4

BEANS

200g Dried pinto beans soaked in lots of water overnight

1 Onion finely diced

2 Leeks green leafy part removed and white part cut in half and cut into half moons

2 Teaspoons of curry powder

1 Teaspoon of garam masala powder

½ Teaspoon of turmeric

1 Tablespoon of maple syrup

1 Tablespoon of vinegar

Drizzle of olive oil

Salt and pepper

Step 1: Drain and rinse the beans and then cook in lots of water over a medium heat until nice and tender.

Step 2: Sweat off the onion and leek until soft and sweet. Add the spices, vinegar, maple syrup, cooked beans and season to taste.

CULTURED CASHEW SOUR CREAM

MAKES 2 CUPS

2 Cups of raw cashews soaked for 8 hours in filtered water

2 Probiotic capsules

Splash of water

TIP

If you want a cheesy sauce add some nutritional yeast after it has fermented. It's really lovely!

Step 1: Drain and rinse the cashews and then blend with a splash of water until smooth. Once it resembles the texture of yoghurt open the probiotic capsules and pour in the contents. Blend for a further 10 seconds.

Step 2: Pour this mixture into a bowl and cover with cling film. Allow to ferment in a warm place for 24 hours.

Step 3: It should smell sour and have lots of air bubbles inside.

Step 4: Season and add chopped chives to serve.

QUESADILLA
Follow the "Chickpea Frittata with Aubergine Bacon, Cashew Soured Cream and Avocado Salsa" recipe for the base, page 113 in the Mains section.

SALSA
Follow the "Salsa" recipe on the "Fully Loaded Nachos" recipe, page 120 in the Mains section.

GUACAMOLE
Follow the "Guacamole" recipe on the "Fully Loaded Nachos" recipe, page 120 in the Mains section.

RED PEPPER WRAPS WITH SMOKED TEMPEH

Serves 4

RED PEPPER WRAPS

3 Cups of chopped red pepper

1 Cup of chopped courgette

½ Cup of chopped fresh tomatoes

½ Cup of sun-dried tomatoes soaked for 2 hours in warm water

½ Avocado peeled and de-stoned

¾ Tablespoon psyllium husk

⅛ Teaspoon sea salt

Step 1: Combine all the ingredients together in a high-speed blender until smooth.

Step 2: Divide the mixture between 2 dehydrator trays lined with a non-stick paraflex sheet.

Step 3: Dehydrate for 6 to 8 hours in the dehydrator (see page 26 for an alternative cooking method).

Step 4: Check the sheets. They should easily peel away from the non-stick sheet by lifting in the corners. Turn them over and dry for another hour. When they are ready, they can be rolled or folded, and stored in a sealable box until ready to use. They will store for up to 3 weeks.

SMOKED TEMPEH

1 Block of smoked tempeh (175g) cut into thin strips

1 Dessert spoon coconut oil

Step 1: Warm the coconut oil in a shallow pan.

Step 2: When the oil has turned to a liquid and is hot, add the strips of tempeh and cook lightly until golden brown.

Step 3: Remove from the pan and leave to cool on a paper towel.

GARLIC SPINACH

4 Cups of washed baby spinach leaves

1 Clove of garlic crushed

1 Cup of soaked and chopped sun-dried tomatoes

½ Dessert spoon olive oil

⅛ Teaspoon sea salt

Freshly ground black pepper

Step 1: Put the 4 cups of baby spinach in a large bowl with the salt and pepper and massage well with your hands until all the water has come out of the leaves. Squeeze out the excess water.

Step 2: Massage in the olive oil, sun-dried tomatoes and garlic until it resembles 'cooked' spinach. Leave in a dry bowl until ready to use.

AVOCADOS

2 Medium-sized ripe avocados peeled and de-stoned

1 Lemon juiced

Slice the avocado lengthways into strips, and put them on a plate. Brush with lemon juice until ready to use.

TAHINI LEMON DRESSING

½ Cup of tahini

1 Lemon juiced

¼ Cup of water

¼ Cup of olive oil

Sea salt to taste

Step 1: Blend the tahini with the lemon juice, water and olive oil until smooth.

Step 2: Pour into a glass jar and refrigerate until ready to use.

TO ASSEMBLE THE WRAPS

2 Handfuls of fresh sprouts (alfalfa, broccoli, sunflower etc.)

Step 1: Cut the red pepper wraps in half so that you have 4 pieces.

Step 2: Lay the spinach on the bottom of each wrap and divide the tempeh strips between them.

Step 3: Drizzle with the tahini dressing.

Step 4: Lay the avocado slices over the top and cover with the sprouts.

Step 5: Roll the wraps and keep the mixture tight, to form long sushi-like rolls. Refrigerate for 20 minutes before cutting and serving.

TIP

These wraps will keep overnight in the fridge. They are a perfect 'on the go' snack!

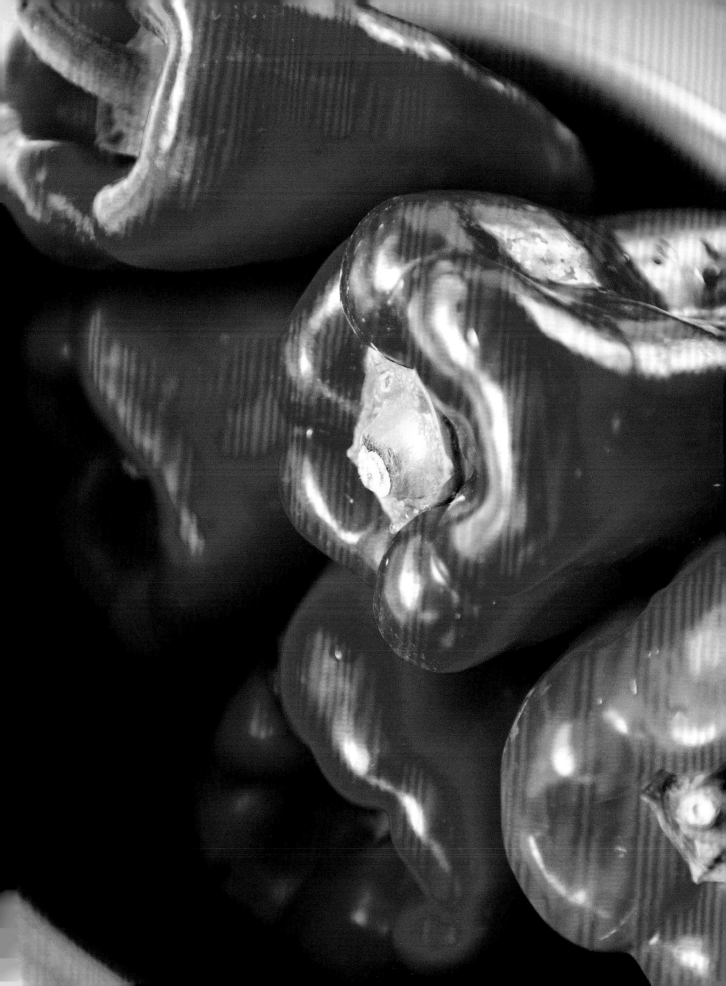

SOBA NOODLES, AVOCADO AND TAHINI SAUCE

Serves 2

NOODLES

100g Soba noodles
1 Avocado sliced into strips or cubes
1 Carrot peeled and grated
4 Spring onions sliced thinly
Sprinkle of black sesame seeds

Step 1: Boil the noodles in water for 2 minutes. Drain in a colander.

Step 2: Add the carrot, spring onions and avocado.

TAHINI SAUCE

2 Heaped tablespoons tahini
½ Inch piece of ginger
1 Clove of garlic
1 Tablespoon tamari
¼ Cup of water

Put everything into a blender and whizz until smooth. Mix in to the noodles with a sprinkle of black sesame seeds to garnish.

SUN BURGERS WITH GRILLED AUBERGINE, PROBIOTIC KETCHUP AND CARAMELISED ONIONS

Serves 4

SUN BURGERS

1 Cup of walnuts soaked overnight in water

1 Cup of pumpkin seeds soaked overnight in water

7 Soaked sun-dried tomatoes, cut into halves

⅔ Cup of chopped Portobello mushrooms

2 Tablespoons tamari

¼ Teaspoon sea salt

⅓ Cup of shredded carrots

¼ Teaspoon chilli powder

½ Teaspoon chopped garlic

3 Tablespoons olive oil

Step 1: Add the walnuts, pumpkin seeds and sun-dried tomatoes to the food processor and process until you have a rough consistency.

Step 2: Add the Portobello mushrooms and mix again.

Step 3: Add the remaining ingredients: tamari, shredded carrots, chilli, garlic, olive oil and sea salt. Process again until well mixed together.

Step 4: Divide the mixture into 4 balls. Press the mixture into a steel ring or cookie cutter on a dehydrator sheet lined with a non-stick paraflex sheet (see page 26 for an alternative cooking method).

Step 5: Remove the rings from your "burgers" and dehydrate for 4 hours at 50°C on one side.

Step 6: After 4 hours flip the patties and dry for another 4 hours.

GRILLED AUBERGINE

8 Thick slices of aubergine

⅛ Cup of olive oil

½ Teaspoon salt

Step 1: Place the aubergine slices on a tray. Score the slices with a sharp knife and sprinkle with sea salt and leave to stand for 4 hours.

Step 2: Rinse the aubergine slices under cold running water and dry on a paper towel.

Step 3: Heat the olive oil in a pan and seal the aubergine slices for about 1 minute each side, or until the aubergine is slightly golden. Remove and place on a paper towel until ready to serve.

PROBIOTIC KETCHUP

1 Cup of organic tomato paste
1 Probiotic capsule
1 Dessert spoon tamari
2 Teaspoons maple syrup

Step 1: Place the tomato purée in a glass bowl with the tamari and maple syrup and mix well.

Step 2: Empty the contents of the probiotic capsule in the mixture and again mix well.

Step 3: Leave the mixture in a warm place overnight to ferment.

Step 4: Refrigerate until ready to use.

CASHEW CHEESE

2 Cups of organic cashew nuts soaked overnight
½ Cup of filtered or spring water
1 Dessert spoon nutritional yeast
1 Teaspoon onion powder
⅛ Teaspoon turmeric powder
Sea salt to taste

Step 1: Put the cashews in a high-speed blender with the half cup of water.

Step 2: Place a large fine sieve over a bowl and sieve the nutritional yeast, onion powder and turmeric together.

Step 3: Add the dry mixture to the cashews in the blender and blend on high until you have a smooth, silky appearance.

Step 4: Add the sea salt to taste and then pour the contents into a glass to refrigerate until ready to use.

TO ASSEMBLE THE BURGERS

Assemble the burgers by placing one of the aubergine slices on a board with some dressed organic rocket leaves on the top. Place the burger over this with a dollop of the probiotic ketchup. Add a little cashew cheese and place the other aubergine on top.

Serve with baked sweet potatoes and salad.

TIP

The 'burgers' in this recipe can be made and stored in the refrigerator for up to 5 days, which makes things a lot less 'last minute' when you're entertaining. You can just drop them in the dehydrator for 1 hour before you're ready to serve.

SUSHI

Makes 2 to 3 rolls

RICE

2 Cups of sushi rice

4 Cups of water

2 Tablespoons raw cane sugar

4 Tablespoons cider vinegar

1 Tablespoon sea salt

FILLING

2 to 3 Seaweed sheets

½ Avocado cut into strips

½ Cucumber cut into strips

Chives

Wasabi to taste

Step 1: For the rice: put everything into a saucepan and bring to the boil. As soon as it starts to boil turn the heat down to low and put a tight-fitting lid on the pan. Allow to simmer for 20 minutes or until all the liquid has been absorbed then rest for 15 minutes. Place into a container ready to use later.

Step 2: For the rolling: place your seaweed sheet shiny side down onto a rolling mat, so you seeing the deep grooves 1 inch apart facing upwards. Prepare a bowl of water to have close by so you can wet your hands, this will stop the rice from sticking to them. Wet your hands and sprinkle a small handful of rice over your seaweed sheet leaving a clear 1 inch strip at the top. Once the rice is evenly distributed press it down with your fingers until the rice layer is about 7mm thick. Make sure it goes all the way to the edges, this will make it easier to roll.

Step 3: Spread as much or as little wasabi as you like 1 inch up from the bottom. A pea and a half is a good measure to go by. Then place the cucumber and avocado along this line with the chives.

Step 4: Lift the mat with your thumbs and start to fold over using your fingers to hold the ingredients in. Keep rolling it over until you can't see them anymore. Lightly wet the top inch of seaweed you left clear and seal the roll.

Step 4: Wrap in cling film and store in the fridge.

TIP

A little confused? You can always check YouTube for a sushi making tutorial.

SWEET POTATO WITH CHIPOTLE WALNUT RAGU AND BASIL YOGHURT

Serves 4

CHIPOTLE WALNUT RAGU

2 Cups of walnuts soaked in filtered water for 6 hours

½ Cup of sun-dried tomatoes soaked in filtered water for 3 hours

1 Clove of garlic crushed

¼ Teaspoon smoked paprika

½ Soaked chipotle chilli

¼ Small onion finely chopped

1 Tablespoon chopped fresh coriander

2 Small tomatoes chopped

Sea salt to taste

Step 1: Place the onions, chipotle chilli and the water used to soak the walnuts and sun-dried tomatoes into the food processor, blend until smooth.

Step 2: Add the walnuts, sun-dried tomatoes, garlic, smoked paprika and chopped tomatoes, and process again until you have a 'roughly chopped' appearance.

Step 3: Put the contents into a bowl and add the coriander and sea salt.

Step 4: Leave until ready to use.

SWEET POTATO

2 Medium-sized sweet potatoes washed

150g Cherry tomatoes

1 Dessert spoon melted coconut oil

½ Teaspoon sea salt

Step 1: Line a roasting tray with greaseproof paper and brush with melted coconut oil.

Step 2: Slice the washed sweet potatoes into long strips and lay them flat in the trays.

Step 3: Wash the cherry tomatoes and cut them in half. Add these to the tray with the flat side facing up.

Step 4: Bake in the oven at 180°C for 30 minutes or until soft. When they're ready, remove from the oven and leave to cool. Whilst these are cooking, prepare the basil yoghurt.

BASIL YOGHURT

1½ Cups of soaked cashews soaked for 6 – 8 hours in filtered water

1 Cup of basil leaves

1½ Cups of filtered or spring water

1 Lemon juiced

Sea salt to taste

Step 1: Put the soaked cashews and water in a high-powered blender and process until silky smooth.

Step 2: Add the basil leaves and lemon juice and process again.

Step 3: Add the sea salt and then pour the contents into a bowl, refrigerate until ready to use.

Assemble using the photograph as a guide. Sprinkle with nutritional yeast and serve with salad.

THAI GREEN CURRY WITH COCONUT JASMINE RICE

Serves 4

THAI GREEN CURRY

800ml Coconut milk of your choice

1 Heaped tablespoon of green curry paste

1 Aubergine cut into 2cm cubes

1 Red pepper cut into 2cm cubes

1 Courgette deseeded and sliced into half moons

100g of mange tout or green beans washed

1 Tablespoon of tamari or soy sauce

1 Tablespoon of coconut sugar

Step 1: Add the coconut milk to a saucepan and reduce it by ⅓ over a medium heat. Don't boil it too furiously, or it will bubble up out of the pan and make a mess (trust me, I've done it!).

Step 2: Whisk in your curry paste then add the coconut sugar and stir until dissolved.

Step 3: Add the chopped aubergine and cook for 5 minutes on a gentle simmer, chuck in the rest of the raw vegetables raw and cook for 2 more minutes.

Step 4: Serve with jasmine rice or your preferred accompaniment.

COCONUT JASMINE RICE

2 Cups of jasmine rice
2 Cups of water
1 Cup of coconut milk
Pinch of salt

Step 1: Wash the rice under cold water to remove some of the starch.

Step 2: Put all the ingredients into a saucepan and bring to a boil.

Step 3: Reduce the heat to low and put on a tight fitting lid and cook for a further 15 minutes or until all the liquid has gone.

TIP

This is one of my favourite dishes ever! You can add all sorts of vegetables to this recipe but I like to use these ones for their beautiful colours and crunchy texture. If you want perfect rice every time you could invest in a rice cooker, they are amazing.

VEGETABLE LASAGNE

Serves 4

THE STACK

2 Red onions cut in half and sliced into thin strips

3 Courgettes sliced 1cm thick

2 Aubergines sliced 1cm thick

Step 1: Lightly pan fry your onions in olive oil, salt and pepper until they start to soften.

Step 2: Grill your courgettes and aubergines on both sides until they're soft and look a little charred. If you don't have a grill, bake them at 180°C for 10 to 15 minutes until tender.

TOMATO AND LENTIL SAUCE

200g Red lentils pre-soaked for 6 hours

8 Ripe plum tomatoes roughly diced into chunks

1 White onion diced into small cubes

2 Cloves of garlic crushed and chopped

1 Tablespoon tomato purée

½ Teaspoon oregano

Olive oil

Splash of water

Salt and pepper

Step 1: Rinse your lentils and cook them in boiling water for 20 minutes. Once cooked drain the water and keep to one side for later.

Step 2: Warm the olive oil in a pan over a medium heat and add the onions and garlic with a pinch of salt and pepper, sweat them off until they start to soften. When they look transparent, add the tomato purée and cook for a further 2 minutes until it starts to catch to the bottom of the pan. Then add the rest of the ingredients, including your lentils. Turn the heat down to low and simmer for 30 minutes, stirring every so often to make sure it doesn't stick to the bottom.

Assemble as shown in the photo. Serve with cashew sour cream (see the "Cultured Cashew Sour Cream" recipe on page 234) and basil pesto (page 256 of the Accompaniments section) and a small bunch of rocket on the top.

WILD MUSHROOM PIZZAS WITH ARTICHOKE AND TRUFFLE OIL MASH

Serves 4

BUCKWHEAT PIZZA CRUSTS

1 Cup of sprouted buckwheat soaked for 20 minutes, rinsed and sprouted (this can take 1 – 2 days, see page 33 for the method)

¼ Cup of olive oil

½ Cup of walnuts soaked for 6 hours in filtered water

3 Medium-sized carrots peeled and finely diced

1 Dessert spoon chopped fresh basil

1 Clove of garlic chopped

Sea salt to taste

Step 1: For the sprouts: place the buckwheat in a sprouting jar covered with filtered water. After a couple of hours, wash them and leave in the jar in a cool dry place. Wash the buckwheat regularly as they can become "sour" if not washed often enough. After a day or two small shoots will appear, when this happens they are ready to use.

Step 2: Place the sprouted buckwheat in a food processor and pulse until smooth.

Step 3: Add the soaked walnuts, process again. Then add the carrots, rosemary and garlic. Pulse it all together until the mixture is smooth. Add the sea salt to taste.

Step 4: Put the mixture onto a dehydrator sheet lined with a paraflex sheet (see page 26 for an alternate cooking method).

Step 5: Smooth the dough into a large rectangular square using a palette knife.

Step 7: Score the mixture into 4 equal squares using a sharp knife.

Step 8: Dehydrate for 8 hours at 50°C and then carefully turn over using a palette knife and dry on the other side for another 2 hours.

Step 9: When dry store in an airtight container until ready to use. They keep for up to 2 weeks, so are perfect for making to keep in your cupboard as a 'go to' snack.

ARTICHOKE AND TRUFFLE OIL MASH

1 Large jar of preserved artichoke hearts in olive oil

1 Small clove of garlic crushed

½ Dessert spoon nutritional yeast

½ Cup of fresh basil leaves

⅛ Cup of truffle oil

Sea salt to taste

Step 1: Drain the artichokes in a large sieve over a bowl.

Step 2: When there is no oil left on the artichokes place in a food processor with the crushed garlic, nutritional yeast and truffle oil and blend until smooth.

Step 3: Put the contents into a bowl and mix the basil leaves in with a spoon.

Step 4: Season to taste and refrigerate until ready to use.

WILD MUSHROOMS

1 Cup of oyster mushrooms
½ Cup of shiitake mushrooms
½ Cup of enoki mushrooms
½ Cup of olive oil
Freshly ground black pepper
Sea salt to taste

Step 1: Prepare the oyster mushrooms by pulling them into strips.

Step 2: Remove the woody stalk from the shiitake and cut the caps in half.

Step 3: Next remove the bottom of the enoki stems and mix in a bowl with the rest of the mushrooms.

Step 4: Heat the olive oil in a large flat pan. When hot, add the mushrooms and sauté until golden.

Step 5: Add some sea salt and black pepper, and then place in a bowl until ready to serve.

SPINACH

4 Cups of organic spinach leaves
Freshly ground black pepper
Sea salt to taste

Put the spinach leaves into a large bowl and massage with the sea salt until all the water has come out of the leaves and it is dry.

TO ASSEMBLE

Place the crusts on a bed of spinach and top with the artichoke mash and sautéed mushrooms. Garnish with sprouts and a of the little basil yoghurt.

Desserts

CHOCOLATE CHIA MOUSSE

Makes 2 generous portions

400ml Coconut milk

½ Cup of cacao powder

3 Tablespoons maple or date syrup

1 Teaspoon vanilla powder or essence

½ Cup of chia seeds

The sports massage therapist on camp gave me some homemade chocolate mousse cake she had made. The mousse was delicious, so I made a couple of adjustments to the recipe and this is the result!

TIPS

If the coconut milk is hard warm it through in a saucepan until it melts and follow the same steps. The only difference will be a longer setting time because it'll be a little warm.

Step 1: Put all the ingredients into a bowl and whisk together until it starts to thicken. This should take just a few minutes.

Step 2: When it's nice and thick, pour it into glasses or bowls and allow it to set in the fridge for at least 4 hours, preferably overnight.

CHOCOLATE AND SALTED PEANUT TORTE

Makes 1 big torte or 6 small ones

CHOCOLATE BROWNIE BASE

Double the 'Raw Chocolate Brownie' recipe on page 169 to make the base.

Step 1: Press the base into a torte case lined with parchment paper as evenly as you can, pressing down quite hard to make sure it is compacted.

Step 2: Once it is ready, pop it into the fridge to firm up.

TORTE

2½ Cups of hazelnut milk or milk of your choice

½ Cup of cacao powder

1 Heaped tablespoon of smooth peanut butter

8 Tablespoons of cornflour

2 Cups of the coconut cream from a tin (you'll need 2 tins)

⅔ Cup of maple syrup

2 Teaspoons of vanilla extract

¼ Cup of melted cacao butter

Step 1: Mix the cornflour in with the nut milk and cacao powder and warm over a medium heat. Then add the rest of the ingredients and stir until they start to simmer and thicken. Stir continuously to prevent it from sticking and burning. Taste check for sweetness and adjust if necessary.

Step 2: Pour over the base and chill for 5 hours.

TIP
This recipe is super versatile and as long as you have the coconut cream, coconut oil, and cornflour in it you can have a play around with flavours. Such as raspberry, avocado and lime, lucuma and maca... the list is endless so have a play.

KEY LIME COCONUT PUDDING

Serves 4

---

2 Large ripe avocados

1 Large dessert spoon melted coconut oil

¼ Teaspoon vanilla powder

⅛ Cup of maple syrup

2 Large limes – use the zest and juice

2 Large tablespoons shredded coconut

Step 1: Peel and stone the avocados.

Step 2: Place them in the food processor with the zest and juice of 2 limes, maple syrup and vanilla and process until silky smooth.

Step 3: Add the coconut oil and mix well.

Step 4: Spoon the mixture into 4 small glasses and chill until set.

Step 5: Garnish with shredded coconut, cacao nibs and small mint leaves.

TIP

Serve as a sweet snack or as a dessert. They will keep in the refrigerator for three days.

LEMON VANILLA CUSTARD AND ALMOND TART

Makes 4

BASE

2 Cups of ground almonds

½ Cup of tapioca flour

1 Tablespoon of melted coconut oil

1 Tablespoon of maple syrup

Step 1: Stir the dry ingredients together, then add the melted coconut oil and maple syrup. I use my food processor to pulse until mixed.

Step 2: Press the mixture into a tart case lined with parchment paper and bake in a pre-heated oven for 10 minutes at 180°C until evenly cooked and golden. It might need a couple more minutes depending on the oven. Set aside to cool.

LEMON VANILLA CUSTARD

½ Cup of lemon juice

½ Lemon zested

1 Cup of coconut milk from a tin

½ Cup of maple syrup

2 Tablespoons of cornflour

4 Tablespoons of melted coconut oil

1 Teaspoon of vanilla

Pinch of turmeric and black pepper (optional)

Step 1: Dissolve the cornflour into the lemon juice in a saucepan, then add the rest of the ingredients.

Step 2: Place the saucepan over a medium heat and bring it to a simmer, stirring constantly so it doesn't stick to the bottom. When it looks thick it's ready to pour onto the base.

Step 3: Pour it over the base and refrigerate for at least 4 hours.

TIP

Don't shake the coconut tin and keep it somewhere cold the cream and water divide. Make sure to use the cream from the top of the can of coconut milk rather than the water at the bottom as this will help to set your custard.

MANGO CHEESECAKE

Makes a big 12 inch cheesecake or lots of small ones

CHEESECAKE BASE

3 Cups of macadamia nuts
3 Cups of almonds
2 Tablespoons of maple syrup
1 Tablespoon of coconut oil
Pinch of salt

Step 1: Whizz everything together and press into a lined cake tin. Pop into the fridge to set.

CHEESECAKE

2 Cups of cashew nuts soaked for 8 hours in filtered water with grapefruit seed extract (optional)
4 Cups of mango fresh or frozen
1 Cup of maple syrup
1 Cup of mango juice
⅓ Lime juice
1 Teaspoon of vanilla powder
2 Tablespoons of nutritional yeast
1 Cup of melted coconut oil
½ Teaspoon of turmeric
3 Teaspoons of agar agar
Pinch of salt and pepper, yes that's right!

Step 1: Add all the ingredients, apart from the agar agar, coconut oil and half the mango juice to a food processor and blend until nice and smooth. Leave the mix in there while you complete step 2.

Step 2: Put the remaining mango juice into a saucepan and sprinkle the agar agar into it. Bring to the boil to melt the agar, this step is very important if you want your cheesecake to set.

Step 3: Go back to the food processor and carefully pour in the mango juice and the agar agar whilst it's whizzing.

Step 5: Keeping the processor running, add the melted coconut oil and blend until smooth.

Step 4: Pour over your base and freeze until hard. Take it out 1 hour before serving, or after half an hour if you're making little ones.

LEMON GEL

MAKES 1 CUP

2 Lemons cut in half seeds removed
½ Cup of date syrup
1 Teaspoon of agar agar
¼ Cup of water

Step 1: Put the water into a small saucepan, bring to the boil and dissolve the agar agar.

Step 2: Blend the lemons and the date syrup until smooth, then add the dissolved agar agar. Pop the mixture into a bowl and refrigerate until set. This normally takes about 1 hour.

Step 3: When it's set, blend the mix until it turns into a gel and use it to garnish your cheesecake.

RED RICE AND MILLET PATTIES

Makes 6 patties

PATTIES

1 Cup of uncooked millet

½ Cup of red or brown rice

1 Teaspoon coconut oil

5 Cups of vegetable stock

1 Small red onion finely chopped

1 Leek washed thoroughly and thinly sliced

2 Large cloves of garlic grated

2 Spring onions sliced thinly

2 Tablespoons tamari sauce

½ Cup of tahini

1 Blood orange or tangerine/satsuma… or just an old fashioned orange chopped in half!

Salt and pepper

¼ Cup of chickpea flour

Step 1: Rinse the millet and red rice, and soak in a pan for a few hours or overnight in the vegetable stock.

Step 2: Bring the pan to the boil, and then turn down the heat. Simmer until the water is absorbed and the grains are tender, this will take roughly 20 to 30 minutes. Check times on the packet.

Step 3: While the millet is cooking gently sauté the onion, leek and garlic in the coconut oil in a wide skillet being mindful not to burn them. After about 10 to 15 minutes squeeze in the juice of half the blood orange and continue to cook until it smells delicious the vegetables have started to caramelise.

Step 4: When the millet and rice are tender and most of the water has been absorbed, take it off the heat and fluff with a fork. Stir in the onions, leek and garlic, the tahini and tamari, and the chopped coriander, spring onion and black pepper. Taste and season, then let it sit for 10 minutes. The mixture should be soft but firm enough to make into patties. If, when squeezed gently into the palm of the hand, the mixture falls apart, add more tahini. This should help bind it together.

Step 5: To bake, line a tray with baking parchment and preheat the oven to 220°C. Grease the parchment with olive oil.

Step 6: If the mixture is too wet, add a sprinkle of chickpea flour and mix in well. Make the mixture into about 6 patties with your hands and place on the tray. Brush with a little olive oil and cook for about 30 minutes

---

SAUCE

1 Cup of fresh coriander

¼ Cup of coconut milk

2 Tablespoons fresh lime juice

1 Small clove of garlic

½ Jalapeño pepper roughly chopped

1 Inch piece of peeled ginger diced roughly

¼ Teaspoon salt

In a high-speed blender, add the coriander, coconut milk, fresh lime juice, garlic, half the jalepeño and ginger. Blend until smooth and silky. Add more jalepeño to taste.

RAW CHOCOLATE BROWNIE WITH SALTED CARAMEL SAUCE

Makes 8 or a really big one!

BROWNIE

1 Cup stoned dates
1 Cup coconut shredded
1 Cup walnuts or pecans
1 Teaspoon of vanilla powder or extract/essence
½ Teaspoon of chilli (optional)
4 Tablespoons cacao powder
¼ Teaspoon of sea salt

Step 1: Blend the dates in a food processor until smooth.

Step 2: Add the rest of the ingredients and pulse until everything is mixed evenly into the date paste.

Step 3: Press the mix into a grease proof paper lined tin or tray and chill for 1 hour.

Step 4: Slice into bite sized pieces or big epic brownies.

SALTED CARAMEL SAUCE

MAKES 1 CUP
⅓ Cup of almond butter
⅓ Cup of dates
⅓ Cup of maple syrup
Pinch of salt

Blend the ingredients together until smooth and keep in the fridge until needed.

TIP

If you prefer a bit of texture in your brownies add the walnuts towards the end so the nuts stay chunky and crunchy. The caramel sauce is a little bit naughty, so don't eat it all at once!

SALTED CARAMEL BITES

Makes 6 bars

BASE

1 Cup of gluten-free oats
1 Cup of ground almonds
1 Cup of cashews
1 Cup of dried coconut
1 Tablespoon tahini
1 Tablespoon maple syrup
1 Tablespoon coconut oil

Step 1: Blend all the ingredients together in a food processor.

Step 2: Press the mix into an A4 sized tray lined with parchment paper to stop it sticking, then put in the freezer to firm.

SALTED CARAMEL

2 Cups of dates soaked in 2 cups of boiling water for 10 minutes
2 Tablespoon peanut butter
1 Teaspoon vanilla powder
½ Teaspoon sea salt

Step 1: Remove the dates from the water and add to your food processor, keep the water to one side. Add the other ingredients and blend until it's the consistency of hummus. If it looks too dry, add some of the water you used to soak the dates in until you reach a nice spreadable texture.

Step 2: Spread the caramel on top of your base, sprinkle with walnuts and drizzle with your melted chocolate sauce, then pop it in the freezer to set.

Step 3: Slice into bite-sized pieces store in the freezer.

TOPPING

¼ Cup of melted coconut oil
1 Tablespoon maple syrup
1 Tablespoon cacao

Mix the ingredients together, drizzle over the caramel and walnuts!

TIP

It's important for the caramel to be completely frozen before you try to handle it or it may break when you tip it out of your tray/mould. It will also be much easier to cut from frozen.

STRAWBERRY, RASPBERRY, COCONUT AND VANILLA PANNA COTTA

Makes 4

400ml Coconut milk

1 Lime zested and juiced

1 Orange zested and juiced

1 Teaspoon vanilla powder

1 Cup of strawberries

1 Cup of raspberries

1 Teaspoon agar agar flakes

2 Tapioca starch

3 Tablespoons date syrup

½ Cup of warm water

Step 1: Add the warm water to the agar agar and give it a mix so it starts to dissolve. Set to one side.

Step2: Add a small splash of water to the tapioca starch and give it a little mix. This will prevent it from clumping up when you add it to the other ingredients later.

Step 3: Put the remaining ingredients into a saucepan and blend with a stick blender until smooth. Warm over a medium heat until it starts to bubble and thicken.

Step 4: When it's started to bubble add the dissolved agar agar and bring back to the boil.

Step 5: Pour into moulds, glasses, bowls and chill for 3 hours or until firm to the touch.

I was playing around in the kitchen and thought I'd experiment with a plant based panna cotta - hey presto!

Sweet Treats

ALMOND BUTTER AND CHOCOLATE FUDGE

Serves 4 – 6

2 Cups of organic almond butter

½ Cup of raw cacao powder

2 Tablespoons raw cacao nibs

½ Cup of maple syrup

1 Tablespoon coconut oil softened

2 Teaspoons vanilla extract

1 Teaspoon sea salt

Step 1: Spoon the almond butter into a large bowl and sieve in the cacao powder.

Step 2: Add the softened coconut butter and maple syrup and mix in the vanilla extract, cacao nibs and salt.

Step 3: Keep stirring the mixture until it's well combined and smooth.

Step 4: Pour the mixture into a cake tin lined with grease proof paper and pop into the fridge to for 2 to 3 hours until hard.

Step 5: When you're ready to serve remove the fudge from the fridge and leave to stand for 10 minutes before cutting into bite-sized bits. For the best results, leave a sharp knife standing in a jug of hot water for a couple of minutes before you slice the fudge. They'll keep in the freezer for up to 3 weeks, which is great as they're a fantastic sweet treat.

APPLE DOUGHNUTS WITH HAZELNUT BUTTER

Makes 8 – 10

APPLE DOUGHNUTS

2 Medium-sized apples

6 Ripe strawberries

1 Small handful of blueberries

1 Teaspoon grated coconut

1 Teaspoon goji berries

Pinch of cinnamon

HAZELNUT BUTTER

2 Cups of hazelnuts

½ Cup of plant based milk

½ Cup of maple syrup

3 Tablespoons raw cacao powder

Vanilla beans from ½ vanilla pod (cut lengthways and carefully scrape the beans with the back of a knife)

1 pinch of pink Himalayan salt

Step 1: Roast the hazelnuts in the oven at 180°C on a baking tray for about 10 minutes. Remove from oven and allow to cool.

Step 2: Once cool, place the hazelnuts in a food processor, discarding the skins and blend until they become gritty. Add the maple syrup, cacao powder, vanilla and salt and blend again, pushing the butter back into the middle of the blender from around the sides.

Step 3: Slowly add the nut milk bit by bit. The consistency should be creamy but not watery.

TO ASSEMBLE

Step 1: Wash and core the apples. Cut horizontally into 4 or 5 thick slices depending on the size of the apple.

Step 2: Smother the apple slices with a generous amount of the hazelnut butter.

Step 3: Slice the strawberries and cut the blueberries in half.

Step 4: Cover the apple slices with fruit, toasted coconut, a sprinkle of cinnamon, and some torn fresh mint.

BANANA SAMOSAS

Serves 4

---

4 Ripe bananas

4 Dessert spoons almond butter

4 Dessert spoons fresh raspberries

2 Dessert spoons cacao nibs

Step 1: Peel the bananas and mix in a high-powered blender until you have a smooth batter-like consistency.

Step 2: Divide the contents between two dehydrator sheets lined with a non-stick paraflex sheet. Spread evenly using a palette knife. See page 26 for alternative cooking method.

Step 3: Dehydrate for 6 hours and then peel them off, turn over and dry for another hour or until pliable.

Step 4: Cut each sheet into 4 long strips.

Step 5: Place a spoonful of the almond butter on the bottom of each strip along with some of the raspberries and cacao nibs.

Step 6: Fold into triangles so they look like samosas.

Step 7: Garnish with shaved cacao butter, mint leaves and fresh berries.

CHOCOLATES

Makes 20

100g Almond butter

100g Cashew nut butter

100g Raw cacao powder

100g Raw coconut butter

100g Date syrup

1 Teaspoon vanilla powder or 1 vanilla bean or vanilla essence

Step 1: Melt the cacao butter in a bowl over simmering water and add the vanilla.

Step 2: Once it has melted stir in the cacao powder.

Step 3: Add the rest of the ingredients and mix until smooth.

Step 4: Pour the mixture into moulds and refrigerate for 1 to 2 hours until hard.

TIP

Use this recipe to exercise your creativity, experiment with different nuts, dried fruits, coconut or whatever else you might like to make different flavour chocolates!

GRANOLA FLAPJACK

Makes 8

---

2 Cups of buckwheat

2 Cups of fine oats

1 Cup of chopped dates

1 Teaspoon of vanilla

1 Teaspoon of cinnamon

1 Teaspoon maca powder

1 Orange juiced and zested

½ Cup of coconut oil

1½ Cups of water

1 Cup of cranberries

2 Tablespoons of almond butter or nut butter of your choice

¼ Cup of maple syrup

½ Cup of milled flax seeds

1 Cup of pumpkin seeds

Step 1: Place a saucepan on a low heat and add the water, coconut oil, dates, almond butter, orange juice and zest, stir until the coconut oil has melted.

Step 2: Add the remaining ingredients into a separate large bowl and carefully stir in the warm ingredients.

Step 3: Spread the mix onto a baking tray lined with grease proof paper and bake for 40 minutes at 150°C or until golden around the edges.

Step 4: Allow to cool then pop it in the fridge to set and go hard. This will make it easier to cut later.

Step 5: Tip it out of the tray, slice into portions and enjoy!

MINT CHOC CHIP BALLS

Makes 20

250g Goji berries

250g Dates, de-stoned

500g Ground almonds or ground seeds if you're allergic to nuts

2 Heaped tablespoons nut butter or tahini

1 Teaspoon of vanilla

10 Drops of food safe peppermint essential oil

3 Heaped tablespoons cacao powder

FOR ROLLING

2 Cups of desiccated coconut

½ Cup of cacao nibs

Step 1: Put the goji and dates to your food processor and blend until they look like soil.

Step 2: Add the rest of the ingredients apart from the coconut and cacao nibs, and blend until fine.

Step 3: With the blender whizzing add a splash of water or nut milk so the mixture becomes wet and soft enough to roll.

Step 4: Roll the mixture into balls and coat them with the coconut and cacao nibs. Place onto a tray and freeze ready for later.

ORANGE AND ALMOND BALLS

Makes 20

150g Goji berries

200g Dates, de-stoned

500g Ground almonds

2 Tablespoons almond butter

2 Oranges zested and juiced

1 Teaspoon vanilla powder or essence

1 Cup of crushed toasted almonds for the coating

Step 1: Whizz the goji berries and dates together to make sticky crumbs or a paste.

Step 2: Keep the orange juice to one side and add the remaining ingredients and to the blender, whizz until they are evenly mixed together.

Step 3: With the blender running slowly add the orange juice until the mixture looks sticky enough for you to roll easily. Add a n extra splash of water if you need to.

Step 4: Roll into balls and coat in crushed toasted almonds.

RAWSE'S PIECES

Makes 10

100g Almond butter

100g Cashew nut butter

100g Raw cacao powder

100g Raw coconut butter

100g maple syrup

1 Teaspoon vanilla powder or 1 vanilla bean or vanilla essence

1 Orange zested and juiced – this is optional

4 Tablespoons peanut butter

Step 1: Melt the coconut butter in a bowl over simmering water and add the vanilla.

Step 2: Add the cacao powder and mix until smooth.*

Step 3: Mix in the rest of the ingredients.

Step 4: Pour the mix into your moulds so each is half full and chill for 10 minutes.

Step 5: Spoon the peanut butter into the centre of the moulds and cover with the rest of the chocolate mix. Pop them back into the fridge to set. Once they are hard, either store them in the freezer or keep them in the fridge.

Chocolatiers believe this takes 100 stirrings to achieve!

WATERMELON JERKY

Makes 10-20

½ Water melon
2 Limes zested and juiced

Step 1: Slice the watermelon into roughly 7mm thick slices as shown in the picture, and place onto dehydrator trays with silicon mats or good thick greaseproof paper so it doesn't rip when you turn it over.

Step 2: You can remove the seeds if you like, but I love the extra crunch so leave them in.

Step 3: Zest the limes over the jerky, then cut them in half and squeeze the juices evenly over the top.

Step 4: Dehydrate for 6 hours at 40°C. Flip over and dehydrate for a further 2 to 3 hours (see page 26 for alternative cooking method).

Step 5: The jerky strips will feel sticky and bendy when they are ready. Store in an airtight container.

TIP

Pop a sheet of greaseproof paper in between each layer of jerky to stop the strips from sticking together when you store them.

Savoury Snacks

BABA GHANOUSH

Makes a good bowlful

2 Aubergines
3 Cloves of garlic
2 Heaped tablespoons tahini
1 Lemon juiced
Salt and pepper

Step 1: Preheat the oven to 200°C. Place the whole aubergines onto a baking tray along with the garlic and roast for 30 minutes or until soft. If needed, another 10 to 15 minutes should do the trick. Allow to cool.

Step 2: Remove the skin and stem from the aubergine and blend in a food processor with the other ingredients until smooth. Season to taste.

TIP

I like to burn my aubergines whole over a flame for a smoky flavour. It takes less time but can be a little messy. Burn from raw over a fire or hot coals for roughly 5 minutes on each side until soft, then follow the same recipe.

MUHAMMARA

Serves 4

2 Red peppers deseeded and roughly chopped
1 Cup of walnuts
2 Cloves of garlic
½ Lemon juiced
1 Good tablespoon tahini
Salt and pepper

Step 1: Roast the red pepper at 180°C for 15 minutes with a pinch of salt and pepper until it starts to soften and colour. While the pepper is roasting spread your walnuts on a tray and lightly toast them in the oven as well for 5 minutes.

Step 2: Once roasted add the pepper and nuts to a food processor and blend with the rest of the ingredients until the mix looks like hummus in texture. Season to taste.

TIP

This is great with oatcakes or with salads, lentils, rice and quinoa.

BEETROOT AND WALNUT DIP

Makes 2 ½ Cups

---

2 Cups of roasted beetroot

1 Cup of walnuts

1 Clove of garlic

1 Sprig of freshly picked thyme or rosemary

Juice of half a lemon

Splash of olive oil

Salt and pepper to taste

Step 1: Wash and chop your beetroot into roughly 2cm cubes and put into a roasting tray.

Step 2: Bash the garlic clove and add it to the tray whole with the thyme or rosemary and salt and pepper.

Step 3: Drizzle with olive oil and give it a good mix to coat the beetroot. Cover with tin foil and roast at 180˚C for 20 minutes until a soft. Allow to cool.

Step 4: Blend the all the ingredients together and serve or refrigerate for later.

TIP

To save time you could use pre-cooked beetroot. I would opt for the plain one so you can add different flavours to it and it won't be too acidic.

This dip is delish with crudité, on crackers and makes a great dressing for a quinoa salad!

CRACK NUTS

Makes a 1 litre jar

2 Cups of cashews

1 Cup of pumpkin seeds

1 Cup of sunflower seeds

1 Tablespoon of fennel seeds

1 Tablespoon of coriander seeds

4 Tablespoons of tamari

Step 1: Put all the ingredients into a roasting tray and mix together until coated in tamari.

Step 2: Roast in the oven at 180˚C for 5 to 10 minutes until golden and the tamari has dried up.

TIP

Check the nuts and give them a stir after five minutes to make sure the tamari is evaporating and the nuts are evenly coated. These are called crack nuts for a reason, eat in moderation!

MUSHROOM AND CASHEW PATE

Serves 4

300g Mushrooms roughly chopped

½ Cup of cashews

3 Cloves of garlic roughly chopped

1 White onion sliced thinly

1 Sprig of rosemary stalk removed

1 Sprig of thyme stalk removed

Salt and pepper

Step 1: Lightly drizzle the mushrooms in olive oil add a pinch of salt and pepper, roast at 180°C for 15 minutes with the thyme and rosemary at. Roast the cashews on a separate tray for 10 minutes or until golden.

Step 2: Pan fry the onion and garlic in a little olive oil with a pinch of salt until it starts to caramelise.

Step 3: Now everything is cooked and ready, put your mushrooms, onions and garlic into a food processor. Blend for a few seconds, add the cashews and pulse a few times for a nice chunky texture or blend until smooth.

PEA HUMMUS

Makes 3 cups

1 Cup of peas

2 Cups cooked chickpeas

1 Clove of garlic

1 Lemon juiced

1 Tablespoon of tahini

Pinch of salt and pepper

Place all the ingredients into a food processor and blend until smooth.

TIPS

You can add the peas in a bit later and pulse the food processor if you'd like more of a coarse texture. Serve on crackers, as a dip for veggies or as part of a big dragon bowl.

SMOKED CHICKPEA HUMMUS

Serves 4

---

2 Cups of cooked chickpeas

2 Dessert spoons tahini

1 Clove of garlic crushed

100ml Filtered or spring water

⅛ Cup of organic olive oil

½ Chipotle chilli soaked in water for 1 hour

1 Teaspoon smoked paprika

1 Large lemon juiced

1 Teaspoon sea salt

Step 1: Place the cooked chickpeas into a food processor and blend with the olive oil, lemon juice and water.

Step 2: When smooth, add the crushed garlic, tahini, chipotle chilli, smoked paprika and sea salt.

Step 3: Blend again and season to taste.

Step 4: Refrigerate until ready to use.

TIP

This hummus will keep in the fridge for 3 to 5 days. Serve with raw corn tortilla chips or buckwheat crackers.

Drinks

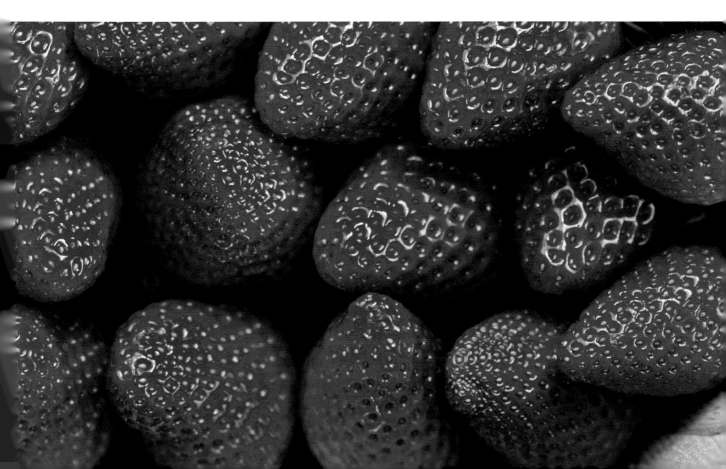

ANTIOXIDANT BERRY SMOOTHIE

Serves 1

1½ Cups of almond milk or dairy free alternative

1 Cup of mixed frozen berries

½ Frozen banana

½ Tablespoon almond butter

¼ Avocado

1 Teaspoon lucuma

A squeeze of lime is good too!

Blend until smooth and drink straight away!

TIP

If you have any fruit or avocado about to go bad and you can't eat them all in time, just chop them up and freeze them! They'll be ready to use at a later date.

AWESOME CHOCOLATE SMOOTHIE

Serves 1

---

2 Cups of dairy free milk of your choice

6 Walnuts

3 Dates

½ Teaspoon bee or pine pollen

1 Tablespoon raw cacao

¼ Avocado

1 Teaspoon nut butter

½ Teaspoon vanilla

Put all the ingredients into a blender and whizz until smooth. Enjoy!

TIP

You can add some maca as well if you like.

EPIC ALMOND COOKIE DOUGH PROTEIN SHAKE

Makes 1 litre

8 Medjool dates, de-stoned

4 Heaped tablespoons of almond butter

2 Tablespoons of chia seeds

1 Tablespoon of bee pollen

½ Cup of pecans or walnuts

½ Cup of oats

1 Litre of almond milk

2 Scoops of protein powder

1 Teaspoon of vanilla

Pinch of salt

Put all the ingredients into a high speed blender and whizz until smooth. BOOM!

TIP

Jam-packed with goodies this shake is brilliant for those looking to bulk and gain!

LUCUMA AND BANANA SMOOTHIE

Serves 1

½ Frozen banana

1 Heaped teaspoon lucuma

1½ Cups of almond milk or dairy free alternative

1 Teaspoon chia seeds

½ Tablespoon almond butter

½ Teaspoon maca

This is one of my favourites! Need I say more?

Blend everything together until smooth. Simple.

STRAWBERRY AND ALMOND SHAKE

Serves 1

1 Cup of frozen strawberries

½ Tablespoon almond butter

½ Teaspoon maca

1 Date

1 Tablespoon hemp seeds

1½ Cups of almond milk or your choice of dairy free milk

½ Frozen banana

½ Teaspoon vanilla powder, essence or extract

Put all the ingredients into a blender and whizz until smooth. Enjoy!

SUPER GREEN SMOOTHIE

Serves 1

1½ Cups of coconut water

½ Banana

¼ Avocado

½ Cup frozen mango or pineapple

½ Teaspoon spirulina

1 Handful of spinach

1 Lime juiced

Put all ingredients into a blender and whizz until smooth.

TURMERIC LATTE

Serves 1

¾ Teaspoon ground turmeric

2cm Piece of peeled ginger

1 Tablespoon nut butter of your choice - I use almond butter

1½ Cups of almond milk or dairy free alternative

½ Teaspoon cinnamon

1 Teaspoon maple or date syrup

1 Teaspoon vanilla powder, essence or extract

Little pinch of salt and black pepper

Step 1: Blend everything together until smooth.

Step 2: Place into a saucepan and gently heat, pour straight into a mug and enjoy!

TIP

If you are using unsweetened milk, add an extra teaspoon of maple or date syrup.

Fermented

COCONUT YOGHURT

Serves 2 to 4

1 Can of full fat coconut milk (400ml)

1 Tablespoon of tapioca starch

2 Probiotic capsules

Step 1: In a saucepan stir the coconut milk and tapioca starch over a low heat until smooth. Take off the heat and rest until body temperature or cooler.

Step 2: Pour the contents of the probiotic capsules into the coconut milk, discard the casing and whisk until thoroughly mixed.

Step 3: Pour the mixture into a clean jar, leave the lid loose and keep at room temperature for 12 to 16 hours to culture.

Step 4: Pop in the fridge to set.

TIP

The consistency of the yoghurt will vary depending on how much tapioca you use, so if you like your yoghurt thick and creamy don't be afraid to add a little extra!

CULTURED CASHEW SOUR CREAM

Makes 2 cups

---

2 Cups of cashews soaked overnight

2 Probiotic capsules

Splash of filtered water

Step 1: Drain and rinse the cashews and blend in a food processor with a splash of filtered water. Once the consistency of natural yoghurt pour in the contents of the probiotic capsule and discard the outer casing. Blend again until smooth.

Step 2: Pour into a clean bowl, cover with cling film and leave to ferment in a warm place overnight.

Step 3: Once fermented air bubbles will be visible, and the mix should taste and smell sour. Season and refrigerate to end the fermentation process.

TIP

If you'd like to add a cheesy twist to this recipe mix in some nutritional yeast once it's fermented.

DOSA

Makes lots

---

2 Cups of basmati rice soaked with 1 tablespoon of fenugreek in water at least 2 inches over the top for 8 hours

2 Cups of white lentils 'urid dahl' soaked in water at least 2 inches over the top for 8 hours

1 Tablespoon salt

Coconut oil for cooking

1 White onion cut in half with the skin still on so you can hold it for rubbing

Step 1: Drain the lentils and rice, keep the water to one side. Blend in a high-speed blender slowly adding the water until the mix resembles a smooth pancake batter.

Step 3: Test the consistency before fermenting. Avoid dipping your fingers into the mix as this is thought to disturb the fermentation process, instead take a small amount on a spoon. It should be smooth to touch, blend again if necessary.

Step 4: Cover with a cloth and place somewhere warm to ferment overnight.

Step 5: When fermented the mixture should smell slightly sour and may have risen a little (don't worry if it hasn't, there will be plenty of bubbles inside).

Step 6: Add the salt and stir with a spoon, you should be able to see the bubbles now.

Step 7: Rub a little coconut oil onto your onion and run it over the pan, warm over a medium to high heat and keep the onion to one side for your next dosa. Once hot put 2 tablespoons of the mixture into the centre of the pan and spread it out using the back of the spoon in circular motions to make a thin pancake. Cook for around 1 minute or until golden then flip your dosa and cook the other side for 20 seconds or less, depending on its thickness.

TIP

Once you've made a couple of dosa you'll have a feel for the method, and you'll be able to whip them up in no time!

KIMCHI

Makes a big jar

1 Chinese cabbage roughly chopped

2 Carrots peeled and grated

4 Spring onions chopped into roughly 1cm chunks

3 Tablespoons salt

COATING

1 Tablespoon raw cane sugar

1 Tablespoon tamari

2 Tablespoons pineapple juice or apple

2 Tablespoons warm filtered water

3 Inch piece of ginger peeled and roughly chopped

4 Cloves of garlic peeled

1 Teaspoon turmeric

1 Whole chilli roughly chopped or 1 teaspoon chilli flakes or cayenne pepper

Step 1: In a large bowl add a layer of cabbage, carrot and spring onion then sprinkle 1 tablespoon of salt over the top. Repeat this until all the salt and vegetables are in the bowl. Massage the salt into the vegetables with your hands and leave to stand for 30 minutes. The salt will soften and wilt the vegetables and draw the water out.

Step 2: Whilst the vegetables are wilting blend the ingredients for the coating.

Step 3: Give the vegetables another mix and leave for a further 30 minutes. Place into a colander and rinse off the salty water, then allow to drain for 5 minutes.

Step 4: Transfer the vegetables into a bowl and mix the coating in evenly. Put the mixture into a kilner jar or something similar leaving a 2-inch gap at the top of the jar. As fermentation takes place oxygen is produced by the good bacteria and the mix will expand slightly. Loosely close the lid so that any excess oxygen is able to escape and leave somewhere dark and dry. Check after 24 hours. Have a taste and if it's not quite tangy enough leave it a little longer. When it's ready, seal the jar and store in the fridge.

KOMBUCHA

Makes 2 ½ litres

FIRST FERMENT

1½ Litres boiling water

1 Litre cold filtered water

1 Cup of organic raw cane sugar

5 Tea bags of tea (black, green, white, etc. not herbal)

1 Kombucha culture "scoby"*

Step 1: Add the boiling water to the tea in a big glass jar and allow to brew for 3 to 5 minutes. If you like it slightly bitter leave it for longer, remove the tea bags when ready.

Step 2: Dissolve the sugar in the warm tea, add the cold water then check the temperature. Scobys don't like to be too hot, body temperature or below is perfect.

Step 3: Add your scoby and cover the top with a cheese cloth or something else organic and natural to prevent contamination and allow it to breathe. Store it in a warm, dark place for at least 5 days.

Step 4: After 5 days your brew will be ready to taste. Slide a paper straw down the side of the jar and plug the top with your thumb. Remove the straw and taste. To avoid contamination don't drink directly from the jar or put the straw back into the brew. It should taste a little sour and sweet, if it's too sweet leave your brew for a few more days before tasting again. Once the flavour is balanced remove the scoby and store it in the fridge or add it to a cup of sweet tea to use again soon.

Step 6: Congratulations, you now have your first kombucha ferment! You can bottle and refrigerate your brew ready to drink or turn over and follow the instructions for the second ferment to carbonate and add flavours to your kombucha.

TIP

*"Scoby" is an abbreviation for "symbiotic culture of bacteria and yeast". I ordered mine online! You can do the same or ask for one from friend who makes kombucha - every time you make a brew another scoby is made too!

SECOND FERMENT

SUGGESTIONS FOR 1 LITRE

OPTION1:

1 Apple chopped

1 Cinnamon stick

1 Tablespoon of maple syrup

OPTION 2:

½ Cup fresh or frozen fruits like strawberries, mixed berries etc.

OPTION 3:

4 Sticks chopped lemongrass

½ Lemon chopped lemongrass

1 Tablespoon of sugar

OPTION 4: FRUIT JUICE

200ml Pomegranate, apple etc.

Step1, options 1, 2 and 3: Place your chosen ingredients into a glass jar and pour in the kombucha leaving a 2-inch gap at the top. Leave for 24 hours, pass through a sieve and pour the brew into a clip-top bottle. Option 4: Pour your favourite juice straight into a clip-top bottle and fill with kombucha leaving a 2-inch gap at the top.

Step 2: Make sure not to fill your bottle all the way to the top as you will need to "burp" your brew later. Seal it and store in a warm and dark place for to 2 to 5 days, the time needed will vary depending on the temperature and sugar content of your kombucha.

Step 3: "Burp" the bottle daily to prevent the build up excess gas and pressure inside the glass bottle (or else it could explode). Be careful, remove the lid slowly and a little at a time. If you see the bubbles rising quickly replace the lid and repeat.

Step 4: When you're happy with your fizz store it in the fridge. This will slow down the fermentation (but not stop it completely). It will last a few weeks chilled.

TIP

Your brew will get better the more you make and as your scobys get used to their environment. Share your extra scobys with a friend or blend into a paste to use as a probiotic face mask!

PROBIOTIC KETCHUP

Makes 1 cup

1 Cup of organic tomato paste
1 Probiotic capsule
1 Dessert spoon tamari
2 Teaspoons maple syrup

Step 1: Stir the tomato purée, tamari and maple syrup together in a glass bowl.

Step 2: Empty the contents of the probiotic capsule into the mixture and mix well.

Step 3: Loosely cover and leave in a warm place overnight to ferment.

Step 4: Refrigerate until ready to use.

SAUERKRAUT

Makes a 1 litre jar

---

1 White cabbage shredded
2 Tablespoons of salt
6 Black pepper corns

Step 1: Chop the cabbage as thinly as possible (I cheat and use a food processor with the slicing attachment). Set the hard white stalk and a couple of whole leaves to one side.

Step 2: Put the shredded cabbage into a big bowl and massage in the salt, pepper and cloves. This will draw the water out of the cabbage. Repeat this every 10 minutes until it feels soft and you have at least a cup of liquid in the bottom of the bowl. This should take about an hour.

Step 3: Pack the cabbage tightly into a glass jar so that it's submerged in the liquid. Use the whole leaf to cover the top of the cabbage and the stalk to help push it down as you close the lid. Leave to ferment for at least 7 days.

Step 4: After a couple of days you should notice some air bubbles starting to form. This is a perfectly normal part of the process however, if we let too much excess gas build up in the airtight container it could cause a big bang and a bit of a mess... don't panic, explosions are easily avoided. Simply "burp" your sauerkraut by release the seal little by little and allow the gases to escape before replacing the lid.

TIP

t should smell pretty funky when ou burp your Sauerkraut. But lack mould forming is a sign to hrow it away (you don't want to oison yourself!).

SRIRACHA

Makes 3 and a bit cups

4 Cups of red chillies of your choice, depending on how hot you like it

4 Cloves of garlic peeled

½ Cup of tomato puree

4 Tablespoons of raw cane sugar

2 Tablespoons of tamari

3 Tablespoons of cider vinegar

Step 1: Blend all the ingredients apart from the vinegar together until smooth.

Step 2: Place the mixture into a jar and cover it with a cloth, nut bag or another breathable fabric. Leave somewhere warm to ferment for between 3-5 days.

Step 3: When you can see little air bubbles and it smells hot and sour your siriacha is fermented. Blend with the vinegar and put it through a sieve, bottle it up and pop it in the fridge.

Accompaniments

ACTIVATED ALMOND BUTTER

Makes a 1 litre jar

1kg Almonds blanched
1 Tablespoon of salt

Step 1: Soak the almonds along with a good pinch of salt in water for 8 hours. Make sure the nuts are fully submerged with at least 2 inches of excess water on top.

Step 2: Drain and rinse the nuts, then dry them in the oven for at least 8 hours at 40°C.

Step 3: Once dry, turn the heat up to 180°C and lightly roast the almonds for 10 minutes. Allow to cool.

Step 4: Blend the almonds in a food processor with a pinch of salt until smooth. Pop into an air-tight container to store.

BASIL PESTO

Makes a small bowl

---

1 Cup of toasted almonds

2 Small bunches basil, be sure to remove those woody stalks

¼ Cup of olive oil or water

3 Cloves of garlic

1 Lemon zested and juiced

3 Tablespoons nutritional yeast

Salt and pepper

Splash of water for texture

Put all the ingredients into a food processor and blend until smooth, or pulse if you like it coarse. If it looks a bit dry, add a splash of water to get the consistency you want.

BUCKWHEAT BREAD

Makes 16 to 20 slices

1½ Cups of sun-dried tomatoes

3 Cups of sprouted buckwheat – see page 32 for details on sprouting

1 Courgette roughly chopped

1 Apple cored and roughly chopped

2 Carrots peeled and roughly chopped

½ White onion peeled and roughly chopped

2 Cloves of garlic

1 Cup of ground flaxseed

⅓ Cup of chopped parsley

Step 1: Blend everything except the ground flax seed together until thoroughly mixed.

Step 2: Transfer into a big bowl and mix together with the ground flaxseed. Blend again in smaller batches to incorporate some air into the dough.

Step 3: Bake for 40 minutes on a greased baking tray at 160ºC and allow to cool

CHOCOLATE CASHEW CREAM

Makes 2 cups

---

1 Cup cashews soaked for 8 hours in lots of water with 2 drops of grapefruit seed extract

1 Cup of nut milk of your choice

1 Teaspoon vanilla extract/essence/powder

2 Tablespoons of maple syrup

2 Heaped tablespoons of cacao

Drain and rinse the cashews and shake off any excess water. Then put all the ingredients into a food processor and blend until smooth. Taste and adjust the sweetness if needed.

TIP

This freezes really well, it's a great idea to batch cook and keep some for another day. It's delicious with the juice and zest of an orange, and makes a tasty sauce when served alongside some banana and berries.

DUKKAH

Makes 2 cups

1 Cup of pistachios

1 Cup of almonds

1 Tablespoon cumin seeds

1 Tablespoon coriander seeds

1 Tablespoon fennel

½ Tablespoon of dried thyme

½ Cup of sesame seeds

½ Tablespoon of salt

Step 1: Toast the nuts and seeds in the oven at 180°C for 10 minutes until lightly golden and allow to cool.

Step 2: Place all the ingredients into a food processor and pulse until it resembles bread crumbs. That's it, ready to sprinkle on salads, curries or anything else that takes your fancy!

TIP

Keep this in an airtight container and it will last for ages. A great way to spice up most dishes.

FLAX AND SUNFLOWER CRACKERS

Makes lots

½ Cup of milled flaxseeds

3½ Cups of water

4 Cups of sunflower seeds

3 Cloves of garlic

¾ Cup of nutritional yeast

1 Tablespoon salt

Step 1: Add 2 cups of water to the milled flaxseeds and give it a quick stir. Allow a few minutes for the mix to swell and turn into a gel.

Step 2: Put the remaining ingredients into a food processor along with the rest of the water and blend until smooth.

Step 3: Spread thinly onto greaseproof paper or silicon mats about 6mm thick and place into your dehydrator at 50°C for 4 hours (see page 26 for an alternative cooking method). Once dry on one side, simply flip over and repeat on the other side. Store in an airtight container.

TIP

If the mixture is too dry you may find that you have to take the lid off your blender and push the mix down. Add a little water until it starts to mix by itself again.

GREEN CURRY PASTE

Makes 1 cup

For the paste

2 White onions sliced into half moons

8 Cloves of garlic

3 Inch piece of ginger or galangal thinly sliced

3 Lemongrass sticks thinly sliced

½ Stick of cinnamon broken up

1 Teaspoon coriander seeds

1 Teaspoon fennel seeds

1 Teaspoon cumin seeds

1 Teaspoon turmeric

For the sauce

400ml Coconut milk

400ml Vegetable stock

Step 1: Fry off the onion, garlic, ginger, lemongrass and seeds in coconut oil until they start to brown and caramelise.

Step 2: Add your fried ingredients along with the turmeric to a food processor and blend into a paste.

To turn your paste into a sauce...

Step 3: Stir the paste into 400ml vegetable stock in a pan. Reduce by half over a medium heat.

Step 4: Stir in 400ml of coconut milk and simmer for 5 minutes. Serve with lots of veggies and rice.

SAMBAL

Makes 1 cup

1 Cup of chopped red chillies

1 Large shallot thinly chopped

2 Garlic cloves thinly chopped

2 Sticks of lemongrass white part only thinly sliced

Thumb sized piece of ginger sliced thinly and diced

2 Tablespoons of maple syrup

1 Tablespoon of apple cider vinegar

Pinch of salt

1 Tablespoon of coconut oil

Step 1: Add a Splash of olive oil to a saucepan and place it over a low heat. Add all the ingredients apart from the maple syrup and cider vinegar and cook until it starts to caramelise.

Step 2: Once the ingredients have softened add the maple syrup and cider vinegar and cook for further 5 minutes or until the sambal looks nice and sticky. Refrigerate to store.

SATAY SAUCE

Makes 1 cup

---

1 Thumb-sized piece of ginger peeled

2 Sticks of lemongrass trimmed

1 Lime zested and juiced

1 Teaspoon maple or date syrup

1 Tablespoon tamari or soy sauce

1 Tablespoon madras curry powder

3 Tablespoons peanut butter

200ml Coconut milk

2 Star anise

2 Cloves of garlic peeled

Blend all the ingredients together until smooth and serve with crunchy vegetables, tofu or use it as a salad dressing.

SMOKEY SWEET CORN TORTILLA CHIPS

By replacing the preservatives often found in snacks like these with mineral rich ingredients and amino acids, we've eliminated any guilt about eating them too. Now that's a real treat!

Makes lots

8 Corn on the cob cooked

2 Red peppers deseeded

½ Cup of flaxseeds milled

1 Cup of water

4 Cups of sprouted quinoa (see page 32 for sprouting instructions)

1 Small onion peeled and roughly chopped

4 Cloves of garlic peeled

1 Cup of activated almonds (see page 32 for activating instructions)

1 Tablespoon smoked paprika

Pinch of salt

Step 1: Add a cup of water to your milled flaxseeds and allow them to swell for 5 minutes.

Step 2: Grill the sweet corn on a skillet pan or griddle until it starts to colour. If you don't have a skillet or griddle pan, you can skip this step. Once cooled slice the corn off the cob with a sharp knife.

Step 3: Place all the ingredients into a food processor and blend until smooth.

Step 4: Spread evenly onto dehydrating trays and dehydrate* at 50°C for 6 hours and turn over to finish for another 4 hours or until crispy.

TIP

*If you don't have a dehydrator roast in the over at 80°C for 1 hour on parchment paper or silicon mats and flip it over to crisp. Be careful not to colour them too much or your chips will taste bitter.

TOMATO CHUTNEY

Makes a large jar

---

1 Large white onion diced into small cubes

1kg Ripe tomatoes diced into cubes

3 Cloves of garlic roughly chopped

1 Red apple diced into cubes

3 Tablespoons apple cider vinegar

¼ Cup of raisins

1 Banana sliced

5 Dates de-stoned and roughly chopped

1 Tablespoon tomato purée

1 Teaspoon smoked paprika

3 Cloves

1 Cinnamon stick

1 Teaspoon fennel seeds

3 Bay leaves

½ Cup of water

Good pinch of salt and pepper

Splash of olive oil

Step 1: Add the olive oil to a pan and sweat the onion, garlic and fennel seeds over a medium heat until they look transparent.

Step 2: Add the rest of the ingredients and simmer for 40 minutes to 1 hour over a low to medium heat, stirring occasionally to stop the mixture from sticking to the pan.

Step 3: Pour boiling water into a jar to sterilise it, discard the water. Transfer the chutney into the jar while it's warm and seal it closed. Keep in the fridge for 2 to 3 weeks.

TIP

With a few tiny tweaks you can turn this recipe into a delicious ketchup. Simply follow the steps above excluding the bay leaves, cloves and cinnamon from the ingredients!

ACKNOWLEDGEMENTS

Firstly, I'd like to thank Sofia for bringing The Body Camp Food Bible to life with her beautiful photographs and design skills. You were a joy to work with.

For the painstaking job of correcting my spelling and grammar I'd like to give a big shout out to Jacks and Kelly, I appreciate that was a big undertaking! Thank-you so much.

And lastly, but by no means least I would like to thank our team at The Body Camp and all of the wonderful guests who gallantly stepped in as my taste testers and provided me with such valuable feedback. Your input was essential in making the final tweaks and adjustments to the recipes in the book.

Ben x